how to start a home-based

Personal Trainer Business

how to start a home-based

Personal Trainer Business

Laura Augenti

Guilford, Connecticut

Library of Congress Cataloging-in-Publication Data
Augenti, Laura.
  How to start a home-based personal trainer business : turn your
fitness passion to profit ; get trained and certified ; set your own
schedule ; establish long-term client relationships ; become the trainer
everybody wants! / Laura Augenti.
     p. cm.
  Includes index.
  ISBN 978-0-7627-5266-9
  1. Personal trainers—Vocational guidance. 2. Personal
trainers—Handbooks, manuals, etc. I. Title.
  GV428.7.A94 2010
  613.7′1072—dc22
                              2009038604

Printed in the United States of America
10 9 8 7 6 5 4 3 2 1

Contents

Acknowledgments

I would like to thank the following people for their assistance and support with this book.

Jerry Santarpia, thank you for everything; your dream, our relentless determination together in business—without you I would not have had this opportunity.

Kellee Warner Lavars, thank you so much; your help is greatly appreciated, and your friendship is cherished.

Ron Riccio, Mitchel Seidman, Ken Reinig, and Andrea Pugliese, thank you for your invaluable knowledge and expertise.

Alicia Adkins, thank you for your insight.

Jim Pullman of Powerhouse Gym International.

Ray Finacchiaro, thank you for your feedback and never-ending optimism.

To my family, especially Mom and Rich and to all of my friends, thank you for your unwavering support and encouragement.

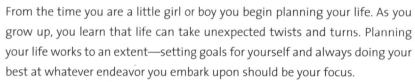

Introduction

From the time you are a little girl or boy you begin planning your life. As you grow up, you learn that life can take unexpected twists and turns. Planning your life works to an extent—setting goals for yourself and always doing your best at whatever endeavor you embark upon should be your focus.

Since you are reading this book, it seems over the course of your life certain events have taken place that have ultimately led to your desire to become a personal trainer and to start your own business (maybe these did not happen at the same time, but at one point or another the two ideas met). Following your dreams and working hard to achieve your goals will set you up for success. But success can have a lot of meanings. Most people, when they first hear the word *success,* think of it in a monetary way: "If I make X amount of money, I will be a success." Sometimes this is true, but you need to look at the big picture. Often, and I have seen this so many times in my own life, people do not follow their dreams; they get "stuck" in a boxed-up world, taking the "safe" route and doing what they are "supposed" to be doing so as not to disrupt those around them.

Following your dreams is something to be proud of. Just the fact that you bought this book and intend to begin the journey to start your own home-based personal trainer business is a major step toward success—and one you should be proud of. You have already overcome the first obstacle. Now, go after your dreams, give them your all, put in your best effort, and give them as much dedication as possible. If you do all of that . . . you will be a success!

I have had dreams my entire life, several in fact. When I was eighteen years old, my sister dragged me to the gym for the first time. Actually, I was a little bit excited to go. I found it energizing, although I did feel a bit inadequate as I took a step class and had no coordination whatsoever! During the entire class

I floundered about. I was embarrassed, but I didn't let that stop me; I took the class again and again until I was good at it. Well, time passed and I tried a lot of different exercises, classes, and so on. Around the same time, my mother started running for exercise; she even did a mini-marathon. So I started to run, too, and discovered that I loved it. Every morning I ran around the neighborhood and sometimes on the track in the park. I also went to the gym to strength train, as I knew how important that was—and I enjoyed it. Fitness became somewhat of an addiction for me, a healthy addiction of course, but nonetheless I needed and craved it.

Helping others is also a strong passion of mine. So when I brought the two together—working in the fitness industry and helping others to become healthy and fit—I was able to satisfy both of my strongest passions.

Whether I was helping a friend train for a marathon, helping a friend lose a few pounds for her wedding, or (big jump) opening a gym on Maui, all were part of fulfilling my dream. Some of these tasks were easier than others, but not much in life comes easy. And, in my opinion, fulfilling your dreams should not be easy; it should in the end be rewarding, but it is not easy.

In addition to fitness and helping others, I had another dream. From the time I was a little girl I had always wanted to be a writer. I used to write poems and short stories, and I always kept a journal. I would write in my journal every day, and I dreamed of writing novels when I "grew up." Life took twists and turns, though, and there didn't seem to be time to write (which we all know is just an excuse). Life was busy, though—opening a gym while holding down another job was very time-consuming. What's more, my other dreams—the fitness dream and the dream to help others—were already in place! So when the opportunity to write this book came along, it was a chance to see my other dream come true. Taking one dream (writing) and using it to continue my other dreams . . . well, that is just the perfect story!

When you look back at your life—no matter what your age—you'll find that certain events led to your desire to start your own home-based personal trainer business. It's a good idea to think about those things. What led you to want to be a personal trainer and, just as important, to want to start your own business? If you feel the passion and are ready to begin, you will do great! Keep focused and keep your mind on your final goal—a successful business that you built with your own mind, your own tools, and your own ambition.

It takes a strong person to start a business, a person with good values, dedication, a strong work ethic (a very strong work ethic), and the willingness to invest the time and effort to turn the dream into a reality. When the chips are down, you have to remain strong and plug through. Every obstacle you overcome will make you a better, wiser, and more successful business owner.

My goal for this book is to give you the tools and knowledge you will need to help you figure out for sure if this is the right business for you, and if it is, what you will need to do to start, build, and maintain your business and be a success! Again, success can have many meanings, and to each person success is measured by different variables. If you persevere and triumph against all obstacles, you will be a success.

In this book you will find information on every aspect of beginning your business, things that you might not have thought of. This book should alleviate and explain some of the obstacles that otherwise you may not have expected. By taking the time to read this book, you are already ahead of the game. You are proving to yourself that you are serious about this business venture and that you are willing to take every step to ensure success.

So You Want to Start a Home-Based Personal Trainer Business?

Jump for joy and pat yourself on the back. You deserve congratulations already! Ambition and drive are the first steps to becoming a successful business owner. By simply picking up this book you're showing the desire to learn what it takes to succeed. Maybe you are currently working in a local gym or as a personal trainer for a small private training facility and feel ready to leap forward and start your own business. Or maybe you are thinking of a *wholesale* career change, and a home-based personal trainer business feels right for you. Well, now is the time!

The demand for personal trainers has been growing, and it is evident that it will keep growing. With the widespread obesity epidemic, the ever-increasing life span, and the overall interest in improving quality of life, it's no wonder personal trainers are so popular today.

Why People Hire a Personal Trainer

Nobody is new to the concept of personal training. We've all seen and heard the many reasons why people hire personal trainers. However, in a gym setting it is easy for the reasons to get lost in the shuffle. Gym members, just by their presence at the gym, have already taken steps toward physical fitness. They'll seek out trainers at the gym. With your own home-based personal trainer business, you will need to be more in tune with your clients and completely focused on their needs and wants. Each person will have his or her own story and different need from you.

There are several reasons why people choose to hire a personal trainer. Here are some:

1. To lose weight

   This is the most obvious reason people want to work out, period. They want to lose a few pounds or maybe a whole lot of pounds. They may have tried fad diets and different workouts over the years, but nothing has worked. Hiring you to motivate and teach them how to work out to lose weight is just what they need.

2. To begin or continue on a healthy path

   When people become seriously ill and overcome that illness, they may become inspired to cherish their health and take better care of themselves so that they can remain healthy and become as healthy as possible.

3. To overcome a plateau

   The majority of people who work out in a gym do the same routine day in and day out. But there comes a time when their body is at a standstill, the progress has come to a halt. The average Joe will not know how to overcome this. This is when a person may seek the help of a personal trainer.

4. To gain motivation

   Have you ever heard people say, "I don't have time," "I was too tired," or "I don't know how to work out"? Well, these are typical excuses for not exercising. For people who lack motivation but truly want to be more fit and healthy, a personal trainer is the perfect remedy.

5. To learn a routine

   Some people have motivation but just need assistance with learning how to work out. They may hire a personal trainer on a short-term basis just to teach them a routine and correct form.

6. To increase confidence

   Many people feel self-conscious in a gym. They feel they need to get in shape before they can go to the gym. While this may sound silly, it is a valid feeling for some people. A personal trainer can help them feel confident in their workouts and will validate them, helping them to overcome their insecurities.

7. To train for a competition

   You might wonder why someone who is fit enough to train for a competition would need a personal trainer. There are many different areas people might be training for: bodybuilding, sporting events, or beauty pageants, to name a few. These people may be looking for a personal trainer to give them that extra boost to get to them to the level of fitness or strength they need.

8. To get ready for a special event

How many times have you heard someone say, "I have to look great for my wedding"? People have many important events during their life that they want to "look better than ever" for, and they will hire a personal trainer to achieve that goal. These people will see a personal trainer for a short-term, quick fix. However, each one is an opportunity for you to get them hooked on fitness so that they will want to continue to look "better than ever" even after their event. The end result is that they will continue to keep you as their trainer.

9. To overcome an injury

Maybe they hurt their knee playing tennis, broke their leg skiing, or tripped over their child's toy and fractured their arm. Whatever the cause, people with injuries are often those who might have been in shape before they got hurt and have lost their shape since. These people often feel their fitness level has digressed so much that they need a personal trainer to help them get back to where they were pre-injury.

10. To make a friend

You may think I'm making stuff up now—well, I'm not, believe me! If a person just went through a rough time in his or her life—maybe a divorce, the loss of a best friend through a tragedy, or maybe a falling-out with a sibling—he or she may want to reach out for companionship. And a personal trainer may be the person he or she seeks out. As a personal trainer, you will spend quality time with clients like this and impact their lives in a positive way. These people will be looking for mental and spiritual enrichment, and physical improvement will be a great bonus for them!

Being Your Own Boss

Wow, it's a feeling of elation—you're free! That may be your first feeling toward the idea of not having to answer to anyone but yourself. But you will soon find out that being your own boss is a huge responsibility and perhaps not as "freeing" as you might have thought. However, if you have the drive and ambition (which you must have, because you are reading this book), you will make yourself a fantastic boss.

Discipline

You've probably said it many times: "I'll do it tomorrow, later, next week . . ." But these are words you are going to have to toss out of your mind if you want to be a successful business owner. When it comes to appointments and other important business matters, you have to have the discipline to see them as important as if you had a boss breathing down your neck, with your job on the line. Because, quite frankly, your job *is* on the line—you are the boss, and the success of your business relies on your commitment.

Drive and Ambition

Starting your own business may sound like a great idea, and it is. But to work, the drive and ambition that you feel right now must stay with you through the process of starting the business, and it must continue once you are in business. There is no room for laziness or passiveness when it comes to succeeding as a business owner and keeping that success growing.

It's All You

When you begin your journey to start your own business, you will realize that decisions ranging from "what equipment should I buy" to "what type of lightbulbs to use" are all your own. While accountability is a good thing because you can create your business completely within your own vision, you must also be prepared to carry the burden of every decision along the way.

When first starting out, you will be responsible for every aspect of your business. You will not only be a trainer, but also a manager, a maintenance worker, and

Working from Home: This Is No Pajama Party

When people think of working from home, they usually picture a person sipping coffee with disheveled hair and wearing fuzzy slippers. This may be true for some home-based businesses, but not personal training. When training clients out of your home, you must be dressed appropriately and groomed neatly. You want your clients to feel as if they are in a professional setting and not as if they interrupted your day.

a bookkeeper. You will most likely see changes in your personality, mainly good changes. You will learn to be a very strong individual, developing skills along the way that you never even knew you had.

Support from Family

Family plays an important role in major life decisions. Having a personal trainer business in your home means you will have people, maybe strangers, coming into your home on a daily basis. Sit down and have a good long conversation with your family—your spouse/partner or parents or children. Find out what, if any, reservations they have. Discuss and come to a resolution before starting your business. Not taking into consideration and respecting the feelings of your family can turn disastrous.

Perhaps you are starting the business with your spouse. The two of you should sit down and discuss the matter of having people coming in and out of your home every day. You may think that since the two of you are in it together, you are both on board with it. Sometimes a conversation can bring out feelings that you did not know were there. It is better to bring out these feelings now and come to resolutions, rather than let them pop up later.

If You Have Small Children

Most people look at working from home as a solution to child care. Let's think about that: How would your clients feel about your two-year-old bouncing on the fit balls during your training session? Most would not be happy about the distraction. When you are a personal trainer, you are being paid to give your undivided attention to your clients during their time, and they want to feel like they are getting the most out of their time with you. To take care of your children at the same time is a nice thought, but one that you should push very far from your mind. Keeping a professional atmosphere is what you need to do to run a successful business, and one part of that is arranging for someone to watch after your children while you work.

Recruiting Family to Help with Your Weaknesses

There will be times when you feel that you are unable to do everything that starting your own business entails. You may be starting the business alone, but you can turn to your family and close friends for support. Is your spouse great at finance? Well then, ask him or her to help you with your budget. Is your best friend an interior designer? Ask him or her for some pointers on how to decorate your studio.

Real-Life Story

When I started my own business, I realized that my organizational skills are not what I would like them to be. I like to use the excuse that I am "too busy" to be organized, but we all know that is just that: an excuse.

My mother happens to be one of the most organized people I have ever met. (I did not inherit that trait, but rather I got my disorganization from my dad. We can't pick what genes we get!)

My mother has been kind and generous enough to help me out; she has been doing my filing for me for years. Every so often she will come over and straighten up my office and file away. I keep saying that one day I will take notes and start being more organized. It's one of those things on my list of "improvements to be made on myself."

Thanks, Mom!

Another good reason to get your family involved in your business is so they better understand how much of a commitment it is for you and how much work is really involved. The best way for your family to understand your business is for them to participate, even if they do the littlest thing, like helping to tidy up at the end of the day.

Running a business all on your own requires you to multitask. You may find you have more weaknesses than you knew as you strive to be organized, motivating (to both your clients and yourself), a bookkeeper, a file clerk, a janitor, a maintenance worker, and so on. Yes, there are a lot of facets to running your own business, so don't be afraid or have too much pride to ask for help. That is what family and close friends are for. The people who care about you will want to support you and help you if they can.

Separating Work from Home Life

One of the biggest obstacles of having a home-based business is not knowing when to stop working. You would think working from home would mean less work, but in fact the opposite is true. If you work at a gym, you train your clients, fill out some paperwork, and then, when there is nothing left to do, leave to go home to spend time with your family and relax. With your business at home, however, you train your clients and do your paperwork, but then you stay at work, where there is always more to do. You might clean up the studio, disinfect the equipment, make follow-up phone calls, update your Web site, write on your blog . . . the list goes on and on. It is very important for your family life, however, to know when to end your workday.

Your Current Clientele

If you have been a personal trainer for some time, you have a base of loyal clients. Now is the time to broach the subject to see if they would be on board to train in your home studio rather than in the gym they are used to training in. (I will discuss the ethics of taking your clients out of the gym and into your home in chapter 9.)

If you are just starting out in the personal training business, think about who you know. Most often your friends and family will be your best promoters. Start talking to everyone you know about what you want to do and you just may be surprised at how many potential clients you have. (I will discuss various ways of marketing and networking in chapter 10.)

In either case, here are some questions you should ask yourself about opening a personal training studio in your home and your potential clients:

- Are you confident that your clients will get just as good of a workout in your home studio as they get at a gym?
- What equipment do you use on a regular basis?
- What is the energy in the gym you currently work out of and will you be able to create a comparable energy?
- Are the clients you have flexible in nature and open to change?
- What are your training techniques, and will you be able to use them as efficiently out of your home?
- What are your clients currently paying per training session? Keep this in mind later when you are figuring out your finances.

Confidence to Build Up Your Clientele

I will talk about confidence over and over again. This is not by accident; it is because from the experiences I have had, confidence is a main ingredient for a successful business. Your confidence will radiate from you and reflect in your personality and training skills. If you do not believe in yourself, nobody else will either. When you approach potential clients, they have to feel as if they will be in good hands. Their time and money are precious, and if you don't seem confident, they certainly will not hire you. So hold your head high and put on a smile—this is your time to shine!

Credibility—You Are What You Do

Whoever said "Don't judge a book by its cover" had wishful thinking. As a personal trainer you have a responsibility to portray the picture of fitness. Your physical image is your first impression to potential clients or to a person who may refer a potential client to you.

Are You Physically Fit?

I wish I did not have to bring up this topic, but it is necessary. When you look in the mirror, do you see a person who is in shape? (Although round is a shape, let's hope that is not the shape you see.) When other people look at your body, are they envious and do they want to get the body that you have?

Personal training is one profession in which it really does matter that you are physically fit. Your level of fitness will have an impact on your success. Now of course it is more important that you possess a wealth of knowledge and experience and can give your clients the tools they need to improve their health and fitness level. However, that first impression is what will give you the opportunity to prove that you are a fantastic trainer and that ultimately you will be worth your clients' time and money.

Do You Live a Healthy Lifestyle?

Along the same lines as looking good, you must also portray a healthy lifestyle. Now you may be thinking, "How could I be looking good if I don't live a healthy life?" It can happen. You may smoke on occasion or like to eat fast food. I am not telling you that you can never again indulge in a Big Mac or eat that turkey leg when you are at Disneyland, but you need to portray moderation and control. Your reputation should precede you as a healthy and fit person who is also human and needs to indulge once in a while.

When you are out in public, realize that everyone around you is a potential client. You want the public to see you making the choices that you would advise them to make as their trainer.

A Home-Based Studio or a Gym: How Clients See It

When people contemplate hiring a personal trainer, many ideas and thoughts go through their mind. It would be nice for you if all of your clients simply wanted to train so that they could be healthier, lose weight, and look good, with no other factors weighing in. However, like most things in life, the reasons people want to hire a personal trainer are not black and white. There are several things that will sway a person's decision to hire you.

Of course your reputation has a lot to do with whether or not someone will want to have you as his or her trainer. But another big factor will be the fact that you train out of your home. Several things go through a person's mind as he or she considers using a trainer who works out of a home instead of a gym. Here are some pros and cons of each option that you should be aware of:

Pros

- **Privacy.** Privacy can be a big issue for some people. The people who do not feel comfortable going to the gym because they feel "inadequate" or too "out of shape" may feel relieved to train where there are no eyes on them but yours.

- **Distractions.** Working out of a home studio will allow your clients to maximize their time with you. In a gym setting there are bound to be distractions. We all know (or should know) that interrupting a trainer in the middle of a session is a definite no-no in a gym, but there are inevitably those who disregard gym etiquette and interrupt you. Or perhaps your client's friend is in the gym and comes over to chat. This takes away from training time and therefore takes away from gaining the ultimate results.
- **"Meat market."** All of us gym rats have heard the phrase "meat market" a time or two. In the 1980s gyms were notorious for being pickup spots, and this atmosphere still exists, probably more than we care to admit—or perhaps today we just know how to talk about it without complaining. However, the meat-market atmosphere is a deterrent for many people thinking about even stepping foot in a gym.

Cons

- **Lack of social interaction.** While some folks might find this a pro, everyone is different. Some people like social interaction, or the "buzz" of others around them, while they train. Having others around may create more energy for these people, so they may need encouragement and possibly more motivation and energy from you than those who are not bothered by the lack of social interaction.
- **Limited equipment.** Training in your home studio will of course limit the amount of equipment you will be able to provide to your clients. Some people may think they won't get as good of a workout as they would in a gym with more equipment. It is your job to convince them that this is not true. Later in this book we will review equipment and how to maximize your options in a small space. Your clients should be able to get as good a workout in your studio as anywhere else, maybe better because they will have YOU as their trainer!
- **Not a "meat market."** Yes, this is both a pro and con. While some people are turned off by the potential pickup line or others "checking them out" while they sweat it out at the gym, some people like it. For some folks, motivation

to get to the gym is to see who is there . . . and maybe even get a date for Friday night.

Personality Traits for Success

If you didn't think being a personal trainer was a personality contest, think again. Believe it or not, your personality may be as important as your skills when it comes to keeping your clients happy and achieving your ultimate long-term goals. You may think you know this from being in a gym setting; you know you have to be likeable. So what I am telling you that you don't already know? Training clients in your home puts a whole new twist on the importance of your personality. When you train

My "Meat Market" Horror Story

Okay, so maybe this is not a "horror story," but it certainly was not positive in my book.

I mentioned in my introduction that I first joined a gym when I was eighteen years old. I won't mention which chain this was, but it was a major-name gym, very popular during that time.

It was a month or two after I joined the gym, and I always went in, did my thing, kept to myself, and left. I was not one to socialize in the gym; I was there to work out and that's it. I socialized plenty away from the gym with friends—you know, when you are supposed to. So one day I was on the treadmill at the gym when this guy came over and got on the treadmill next to me. He started making small talk, and I answered, but I was short with him, obviously not trying to continue the conversation. Finally I got fed up, because he was so persistent and wouldn't stop talking to me. I cut my workout short and was going to leave, but first I sat down to tie my sneaker. He sat down next to me! How mad do you think I was? Well, I was so pissed off that I finally walked out and did not return to the gym for a couple of months (I believe that is when I started running).

Now, granted, I was eighteen years old, and maybe things bothered me too much back then. Today I would tell him where to go . . . and continue my workout, never thinking twice about it. But my point is that some people really despise the "meat market" feel of the gym.

Eye Candy!

When I owned the Powerhouse Gym on Maui, I was often asked, "When is the best time to come to the gym to see the hot guys/girls?" I always laughed in response, but it was a real question. There are many people out there who use the gym to meet people. On one hand, it's a great place to form new friendships, because the people there are interested in taking care of themselves—which is always a good trait!

I have personally witnessed guys and girls making really good friends at the gym, as well as beginning romantic relationships.

Your clients will be in the seclusion of your home, however, and some may really like this. Others, or maybe even most, will go to a gym in addition to training with you.

clients in your home you no longer have the energy of a gym setting and a mix of people to take some of the pressure off of you. In a gym your clients spend time with you, but there are also a whole bunch of other people around. The tone of the gym plays a big part in boosting your personality.

When you train clients at a home studio, however, they no longer have anything to focus on but you! So, here are some personality traits you'll need to have to realize success:

- Motivation. Your home-based clients will need you to turn up the motivation. You will not have the energy of the gym and others working out to feed off of. It will be solely up to you to keep your clients motivated.
- Patience. Your clients will notice a lot quicker if you start to lose your patience with them. Keep an even temper and avoid being noticeably agitated if your client is not working as hard as you would like, or if he or she is chewing your ear off about his or her son's graduation.
- Flexibility. Being flexible is not always easy. You will own your own business and with that comes control, right? Not always. You may plan your day and have it perfectly set when the phone rings. A client needs to cancel. Then the phone rings again. Another will be late. Many things like

this will happen to throw you off schedule. Learn to be flexible without it ruining your day or hindering your attitude when you are with your clients (who showed up!).

■ Energy. No one wants a personal trainer who lacks energy. Your energy level will definitely impact your success as a home-based personal trainer. It is your job to make your clients look forward to coming to your studio because being there makes them feel good. Your energy should be infectious.

Real-Life Story

I used to live on the island of Maui, a small island. The town I lived in is so small that you cannot go to the supermarket or post office without having a conversation with at least five different people. The personality that Jerry exuded at the business we shared was and is completely infectious. His clients love his energy level and the entertaining way he interacts with them, and they spread the word about him. People in town come to the business just so they can spend time with Jerry. He gives them energy and puts a smile on their faces. Sometimes giving them that smile is worth more than a toned bicep!

A Kaleidoscope of Clients

You already know from your experiences as a trainer or from watching trainers in action that your clients are all different. As the proud owner of your home-based business, you will have to make decisions that will keep your business and your reputation as golden as possible.

When potential clients contact you, you should set up an initial meeting to discuss their individual wants and needs. If you find out that a potential client has a specific condition that could affect how you would work with them, you must make an educated decision on whether you are properly trained to handle the client. In such cases, you have two choices:

1. Explain that you are not trained in his or her specific need (you can refer him or her to someone else if you know of a trainer who is specially trained).

2. Start studying! Get yourself trained so that you can train this potential client with confidence.

Special Populations

Life would be a lot easier if all your clients were in perfect health, twenty-five years old, strong, and active. However, you would probably be looking for a different profession if that were the case.

People of all shapes, ages, and sizes and with a variety of health conditions will come to you for help. In a gym, the head trainer can assign each client to the trainer who is most knowledgeable about the client's specific needs. This will not be an option for you when you have your own business. Again: It's all you!

Here is a list of special-needs clients who might come your way as a personal trainer:

- People who are in a wheelchair
- Pregnant women
- Seniors
- People with heart problems
- People who are physically impaired
- People who have a temporary injury
- Children

As you look at this list, think about the special needs of each client and then decide if you want to invest the time and money it would take to get yourself trained to handle these situations. If you are prosperous enough to turn these potential clients down, that's fine. I am going to suggest from experience, however, that you seriously consider pursuing the training necessary to feel comfortable in accepting these special populations as clients. This should be taken very seriously, though. Do not attempt to train a client with limitations that you have no experience with. Doing so is a liability and an invitation for a lawsuit. What's more, it is unethical and just not a nice thing to do, as you can seriously injure someone.

Children and the Need for Exercise

More and more children are obese, and obesity has become a global problem. Gone are the days of children playing ball in the street. These days they are more likely to play video games while sitting on the couch. Fortunately, many parents are hiring personal trainers for their children. Some teens work with a trainer to help improve their skills in sports; in fact, this is a common reason why many children see a personal trainer. Parents consider personal training an investment, as their child could get a sports-related college scholarship if they become good enough.

If you work with children and/or teens, you need to decide what ages you will accept, and if a child is under eighteen years old, whether you will require the parent or guardian to stay during training sessions. Also, should you decide to accept children and/or teens as clients, you should study up on the topic. The keys to having a successful personal training business are experience and knowledge. There is always more to learn, so keep reading, researching, and studying.

A Multifaceted Profession

You know your clients will want more from you than just help getting in shape. Clients will also use you as a sounding board, talking about how their husband leaves his socks on the floor or complaining about their mother-in-law. When you train out of your home, your clients will talk even more. Training sessions out of your home studio are uninterrupted; there will be no distractions or topics of conversation created for you. Your clients will have your undivided attention.

You might not think this is a big deal, but it is. You will have to respond to your clients in a manner that does not make them feel uncomfortable or as if you don't want to hear what they have to say. Now, by no means am I saying you need to study psychology, but you should realize that just listening is a good start. Your clients will rely on you to hear what they have to say and to validate their feelings. You don't have to—nor should you—give advice or solutions to their problems. Your body language will show your feelings, so keep that in mind. Do not roll your eyes or sigh. If you make clients feel as if they are a nuisance, then you might as well mark them as a loss, because they will look for a trainer with a better bedside manner.

Here are a few ways you may be perceived by your clients, not on purpose but subconsciously:

- friend
- marriage counselor
- therapist
- doctor

This is all par for the course. You will get used to it and know how to handle it. The key is to keep a positive attitude—always. It is important, however, that you not fall into the same pattern as your clients do. In other words, never complain or bring up your own personal woes to your clients. Keep your part of the conversation general and light. For example, it is okay to speak about the weather or make general comments about your family, such as, "My wife and I went to that new restaurant Saturday night" or "My son is graduating kindergarten this June." Keep family or personal complaints and negative comments about life or the world out of the conversation. Your studio should always be a positive and stress-free environment for your clients, a place they look forward to coming to.

Two Bonuses: Experience and Knowledge

Experience is the key to a successful business. You will come across hundreds or even thousands of different injuries, ailments, limitations, personalities, body types, levels of strength, and so on. For each situation, you can and should research, study, and read up, but the one thing that over time will make you the best is experience.

Each client that you work with will leave you with that much more experience. Pay attention to each situation, and think of it as a learning experience for yourself. As you already have some, maybe a lot of experience, reflect on your experiences and begin creating a mental library.

Are You an Established Personal Trainer?

How many clients did you train this week? How many have been training with you consistently for over six months? Do people come to your gym and ask for you? These are questions you should ask yourself now, as you contemplate starting your own business. Think about how established as a personal trainer in your community you are. If you have a handful of loyal long-term clients, you have a good start. The more loyal clients you have, the easier it will be for you to start your business. All business owners start from the bottom and work their way up, but it makes it a lot easier if you have a solid client base to begin with.

Do You Have a Professional Support System?

When you are not with clients, you can seek all the support you need, from fellow trainers, online, from family members, from friends, and so on. What you might miss is on-the-spot support. When you are training clients out of your home and a situation arises, such as a question about a training technique or stretch, you will not have an immediate support system to consult as you would while training at a gym. This is an example where experience is key. The more experience you have under your belt, the more comfortable and confident you will be on your own. You can take that experience you have been building and turn it into your dream!

During the Transition

Chances are you currently have a job working for someone else. Starting your own business will be no easy task. It will be time-consuming, as well as challenging. I would recommend that you keep your job as long as possible while getting your own business started. You may feel like this will prolong things, and you are right. More than likely, going to work every day will prolong the opening of your business, but it is still a good idea. The pressure and stress of not having an income can be too much; it can make the whole process too difficult as well as cause financial hardship.

Perhaps you are thinking, "I will quit my job and focus on getting my business started, because I have enough money saved to pay my bills for two months during this transition." Okay great, but working at your existing job is not the only thing that can cause delays in opening a business. Here are some "what ifs" you need to also consider:

- *What if* you run into obstacles that prohibit your opening in two months and it takes four months to open?
- *What if* something unexpected happens that causes you to spend your reserved funds (your car breaks down, your water heater breaks, or some other emergency)?
- *What if* you don't have the clientele you expected when you first open?
- *What if* you underestimated your start-up costs?
- *What if* it takes six months—or even longer—to open?

I am not trying to scare you; opening a business brings about many emotions and requires a lot of focus. It is exciting, fun, scary, difficult . . . all of this and more. I am just trying to prepare you for the unexpected as much as possible. The more focused you are and the closer you pay attention to this book, the better your chances of avoiding problems. You are already on the right path—you're reading this book, aren't you?! So don't worry, work hard, and have fun. Focus on the end result and the overwhelming feeling of accomplishment you will have—it's amazing!

Basically what I am saying is this: Keep your paycheck from your existing job as long as you can. If this is the reason it takes you longer to open your business, that is fine. This reason is acceptable and reasonable and won't cause any harm. As long as you have a paycheck, it won't matter whether your business opens July 1 or September 1.

Frequently Asked Questions

Here are some questions I am often asked about opening a home-based personal trainer business:

1. How many years' experience do I need as a personal trainer to start a home-based studio?

   This is an important question, because in order to start your own home-based business you have to have experience as a personal trainer. If you do not have this experience, you should think about working at a fitness center or gym for a while—or start networking now! When you are certified and continue to study and research beyond your certification (continuing education), you will be one up on the average personal trainer.

2. I'm a little unsure of myself. Do I have the confidence and drive to pursue my own business?

   Being a business owner requires a whole lot of confidence and emotional strength. There will be many times when you will feel like it is too hard or that maybe it won't work, but your confidence and ambition will keep you motivated and drive you to success.

3. What if I don't have adequate space in my home?

   You have to have space for your home business. Think about where you would be able to set up a training facility (or studio as we like to call it) and whether or not you have a space large enough to create a successful business. (We will talk more about designing a space in chapter 2.)

4. Do I really need a ready client base to start off?

   It is never a good idea to start a business without any clients to start you off. This stems back to your experience and how many clients you have now. If you are a great trainer, and we are sure you must be, your clients will be loyal and follow you.

5. Will my family be supportive of my clients coming into our home?

   If you live alone, then no worries on this question. But if you have a family or even a roommate, you need to consider everyone's true feelings before moving forward on this endeavor. Have a serious conversation with your family to make sure that everyone is supportive of your dream of your home-based personal trainer business.

Make Sure a Home-Based Business Is Permitted in Your Home or Apartment

Before you go any further with your home-based business, you need to check the zoning laws in your town or neighborhood. I would highly recommend that you contact your city or town hall and get a copy of the zoning laws. If you find it is not legal to operate a home-based business in your home or apartment, don't give up hope yet. No, I do not mean break the law! Instead, call a lawyer who specializes in zoning. He or she may know legal ways around the zoning laws.

Once you are aware of the laws and know that you can have a home-based business, do not put this issue to bed. Always keep up-to-date with any changes or amendments that may occur. You can do this by joining your local chamber of commerce or Rotary Club—and actually going to the meetings. You can also stay abreast of changes by reading the business section of your local newspaper.

Homeowner's Association

If you live in a private community or neighborhood that has an association or board, check with them as well as with your town or city to see if home-based businesses are allowed. Many neighborhoods or private communities (including condominiums) have their own set of rules and regulations.

Contact the president of the board or homeowner's association. If you are renting, you may not know who this would be. Check with your landlord for this information.

Full-Time or Part-Time?

Before starting your own business, it is important to think seriously about whether it will be a full-time or part-time job for you. More than likely your ultimate goal will be to have your business be your only job.

Here are a few questions to ask yourself when choosing between full- and part-time:

1. How much money do I need to survive each month?
2. How many clients will I realistically start out with, and how many sessions per month will each client average?
3. Will my partner or spouse be willing to pick up the slack in order to allow me to focus 100 percent on growing my business?

Whether you work full- or part-time will most likely boil down to how much money you need to make each month to survive. Maybe you have saved up a nice nest egg that will carry you through the first few months. That of course would be the ideal situation, but in the real world, that is not likely to be the case. Of course on the other hand, you do not want to spend your life's savings to survive through the beginning of your business. (We will discuss money issues in depth in chapter 7.)

Working Up to a Lucrative Business

You have thought about whether to start your business full- or part-time. Now you need to think about growing your business so that it is lucrative. Sure, I know you want to help people stay healthy and fit, but in the long run, you are probably not looking to work for charity (unless, of course, you are filthy rich!). If you are looking to start a home-based personal trainer business as a side job, that's fine. However, you may want to build your business to a point where it can support your lifestyle, and only you know if you have a modest or extravagant lifestyle and how much you need to sustain it. I admittedly like the finer things life has to offer—fine dining, traveling, designer clothes—so I am constantly trying to build my business!

I will cover advertising and marketing later in the book, but for now I want you to keep in mind that you will always want to work on building your clientele base so that you can have a steady flow of income that can support your lifestyle.

Popular Training Times

If you are already a personal trainer, you have probably noticed that the majority of your clients want to train either early in the morning or later in the evening. This can be tough when trying to schedule your clients' sessions, as obviously you cannot book more than one client at 8:00 a.m. (unless of course they are together and want couples training).

It may end up that you have two or three sessions in the morning and then two or three in the evening. This leaves you with hours of free time during the afternoon. You can choose to do a number of things with this free time. You can get another job, which is a good idea if you absolutely need the money. If you do not have to get another job, you can use the time to build your business. Go out into the community and make yourself known. Volunteer, network, or even stay in your office and work on online networking and advertising ideas.

A Dedicated Space for Your Studio

There is no doubt about it: You need a dedicated space for your home-based personal trainer studio. If you have your studio in the middle of your living room, along with your couch, a stack of Disney movies, and your children's toys, well, that is not going to show your clients that you take your business seriously. You want your clients to feel like they are important and your only focus while you are training them. Your studio should have the look and feel of a professional studio dedicated to working out.

Here are some examples of where you could set up a studio in your home:

- The garage. If done nicely, a garage can be a perfect place for a studio. When you create a studio in your garage, however, you have to be careful that it is not a replica of a workout room from the 1980s. (If you are old enough to remember the 1980s, you know what I mean.) In case you don't know what this means, let me explain: The garage should be transformed into a finished room, one that makes people feel as though they are in an interior room, not a garage. If your garage has a side door from the outside, all the better. One potential obstacle for a garage studio is the weather. You may need to add air-conditioning or heat.
- Great room or family room. This type of room is a good idea if you have a separate living area for you and your family. Be sure to consider the rooms your clients will have to walk through to get to this room.
- Spare bedroom. This room is a tough one, most likely the least ideal. However, you might have a home that has an extra master suite, or you may use a smaller room for your bedroom and use the master suite for your studio. (Good luck getting your spouse or partner to agree to this, however.)

What to Consider for Your Studio

There are several elements to keep in mind when coming up with the perfect plan for your studio's location, setup, and design. Consider the following when making decisions.

Private

When I say private, I mean separate from your living areas. The area should be dedicated strictly to your studio. If you are fortunate enough to have a set up where you can have a private entrance/exit to your studio, all the better.

Professional

I mention this again and again, because it is important that you create a professional environment. You are expecting your clients to come in and pay you for an hour of your dedicated time to professionally train them. The more professional your environment, the more credibility you will have. What I mean by professional is this: Have a studio that is organized, clean, and 100 percent dedicated to working out. Do not have anything in the room that is not a part of your studio (again, no Disney movies, toys, and so on).

Practical

The space for your studio must be practical. Be sure you do not need the space as a "living area." An example of an impractical space would be the master suite if your spouse has not agreed to using it or your family room if your children have no place else to watch TV. You will also want to be sure there is a bathroom close enough to the room you choose. If the nearest bathroom is on a different floor, or through all the living space, this is not ideal. *Practical* can also mean making sure the space is large enough.

Other Questions to Ask about Each Potential Space

- What other rooms will my clients have to walk through in order to get to my studio?
- Is there a door on the room to close it off from the rest of my home?

Suggestions for an Efficient Layout

Put your dumbbells on racks—or better yet, purchase interchangeable dumbbell sets. You will need only two of these, so they will save you space and money! However, when deciding if these dumbbell sets are the right choice for you, consider that they are time-consuming. If you use dumbbells frequently, this may become inconvenient and waste precious training time.

Hang fit balls from racks on the wall to free up floor space.

Purchase a multifunctional adjustable bench with wheels so you can do multiple workouts from just one bench instead of having to find space for a flat and incline bench.

For small accessories, you can get crates or stackable storage cubes.

- Is the room large enough for the purpose?
- Does the room have adequate air-conditioning and/or heat?
- Where is the bathroom in proximity to the room?

Creating a Layout

You want your studio to be both efficient and visually inviting. To achieve this, you need to think about and then carefully plan the layout of the room.

Efficiency

Measure the room to see how much square footage you have to work with. This is important because the amount of space you have determines how much equipment you will order, as well where everything will go in the room. You will need to think about where to hang mirrors (mirrors should be hung on a wall with no windows), as well as where to place your office space (if it will be located in the same space as your studio). You will have to decide where to put your cardio equipment, bench, and dumbbells.

Once you know the square footage of your space and have created a floor plan, review it to make sure the layout is efficient. When a client comes to train, you want to be able to do so in an orderly fashion. You don't want clients to have to jump over equipment or avoid tripping hazards.

Functionality

Your layout should "flow" nicely and easily. You know how you train your clients, so if your routine calls for certain pieces of equipment after others, have them set up so that you aren't going from one end of the room to the other and back again. Granted, each session may vary, but in general, set it up to flow as easily as possible. You may have to perfect this with trial and error over a few weeks or months; that is okay. You will eventually see what works best for your training style and for the ease and comfort of your clients.

Safety

Along the lines of flow comes safety. You do not want your studio to become a safety hazard, so you must be careful and attentive to the details. If your floor plan does not flow smoothly, it could be a potential safety hazard. You want to keep the floor

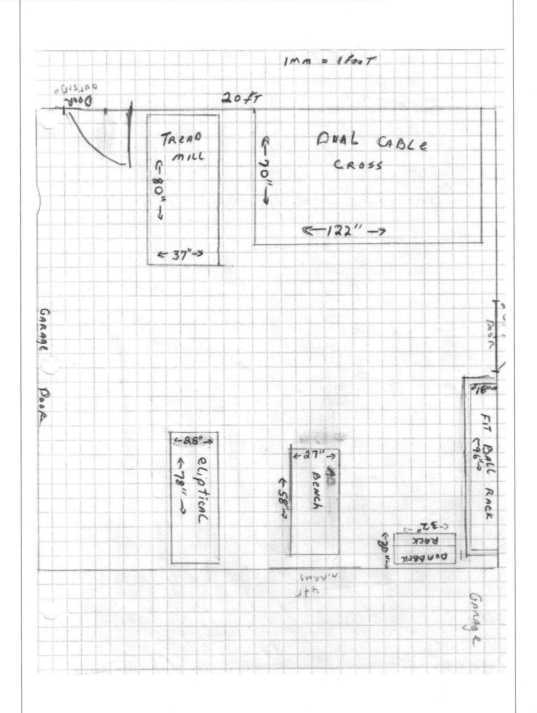

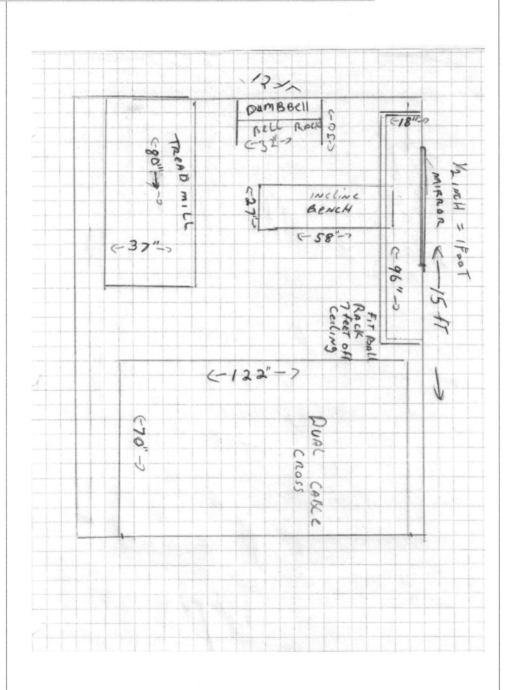

Make It Flow

This is what I mean by *flow:* If you have your clients doing interval training, such as bicep curls and lat pull-downs for their back, you will not want them to have to climb over anything to get from one exercise to the next. There are so many combinations of exercises, which is why it may take some careful thought and planning to arrange your studio.

Before setting up your studio, create a floor plan in your head, considering your training style, how much floor space you will need for stretching, what exercises you like to have your clients do, and so on.

Draw up a few sketches (in pencil) and go through the routines in your head. This will help you to visualize the flow.

as open as possible, and keep accessories off the floor where you can. Preventing injuries and potential lawsuits should be a top priority.

There are several things you can do to avoid safety hazards. Purchase some bins and hooks to keep accessories, including medicine balls, small dumbbells, and resistance bands, off the floor and in a safe place. It's also a good idea to clean up as you go. This will take only a couple of seconds as long as you are efficient and consistent with it. Think about it: What would it take to hang a resistance band on a hook when you're finished with it? One second, maybe two. On the other hand, you can leave it on the floor and watch your client (or yourself) trip over it. Take the second to hang it up; your clients will appreciate your concern and enjoy training in an organized and safe studio.

Visually Inviting

There are many elements to creating a visually inviting studio. For one, your studio should have good lighting. Your clients should not have to squint to see their reflection in the mirror. However, keep in mind that the lighting should be bright enough, but not too harsh.

Another thing to keep in mind is your color scheme, which includes the color of the wall paint, the floor color, posters, and the color of your equipment and accessories. All of these must be weighed together when making color choices. For example, if you order white equipment with red upholstery, you should probably avoid green walls.

How you make your studio come together so that it is visually inviting will depend on your personal decorating preferences and even where you live. If you live in the countryside with mountains and streams, you will create a different theme than if you live on a tropical island.

You are setting a stage for your clients. Part of keeping a visually inviting studio (regardless of the decor) is to keep it neat, clean, and organized. Your studio should look the same for your last client of the day as it did for the first. This will go a long way in building your image, helping you to keep existing clients and acquire new clients.

Keeping Up with the Latest Trends

You may not think about trends when you think about opening your own home-based personal trainer business, but you should. The more versatile your home-based training is, the more you will keep your clients paying you! There is always a hot new exercise gadget or form of exercise that is currently "all the rage." If you live in a city like Los Angeles, these latest trends will be right in front of you. If you live in a more remote area, you will need to do your research to keep up.

Real-Life Story

Living on the Island of Maui, I thought our fitness facility should have an island feel—that if you are on Maui, you should feel like you are on Maui—even if you are lifting dumbbells or sweating on an elliptical trainer. So I had this idea to paint a mural on an entire wall. I found an artist with experience in painting large murals (a friend of a friend) and then I brought him to one of my real-life favorite spots, which has an incredible view of the Pacific Ocean with palm trees and neighboring islands nearby. The artist took a picture of the scene I wanted and then painted that scene on our wall.

Fitness Niches

Targeting different niches can have a positive effect on your business. It is one way to get a wider range of folks interested in what you have to offer. There are fitness niches that have been around for ages, such as running, swimming, circuit training, and cardio classes. And there are others that have become popular only fairly recently. You would be cutting yourself short if you did not take advantage of some or all of the latest niches listed below. What's more, you can target these (and any others you want to) in your advertising and marketing. However, always get some training in each niche before you begin to offer it. You don't have to be an expert, just achieve a level where you feel completely confident as you work with your clients.

Yoga

Yoga has become incredibly popular. The benefits of yoga, from creating long, lean muscles to achieving spiritual balance and healing, have made this form of exercise quite fashionable! Even if you are not trained to teach yoga, you can become experienced enough with it to be able to incorporate aspects of it into your training sessions. Think about clients you have who love to take yoga classes. They may get a boost of confidence in their sessions with you if you incorporate yoga into their workouts.

Later on, when I talk about expanding your business, you might even want to consider offering small group yoga classes. If you are lucky enough to live in a beach community, yoga on the beach has become very popular.

Physical Benefits of Yoga

- Muscle tone
- Flexibility
- Strength
- Improved breathing

Mental Benefits of Yoga

- Stress reduction
- Increased state of mental calmness
- Relaxation

Pilates

Pilates is right up there with yoga in popularity. I cannot count as high as the number of times I have read about Jennifer Aniston doing Pilates. Who wouldn't think Jennifer Aniston has a spectacular body? Pilates obviously works!

Physical Benefits of Pilates

- Long, lean muscles
- Strong core
- Stronger, more flexible spine
- Postural alignment
- Strong abdominal muscles

Mental Benefits of Pilates

- Stress reduction
- Tension relief
- Increased energy

Boot Camp

Boot camp–style exercise classes have become increasingly popular. This intensive full-body workout used to be offered only in group settings out in the park or on the beach. However, like all things, boot camp has evolved and has become much more versatile.

There are many ways to form a boot camp indoors in your studio. You can use circuit training and a wide variety of accessories, including the following (prices are approximate and will vary):

- Cones ($2 each)
- Steps ($100)
- Medicine balls ($20–$60, depending on weight)
- Indoor agility ladders ($50)
- Agility rings ($50 for a set of twelve)
- Power plyo boxes ($350/set)
- Slide board ($550)

These accessories can be purchased from:

- www.power-systems.com
- www.warehousefitness.com
- www.2ndwindexercise.com/shop/accessories/balance-stability-steps
- www.healthstylesexercise.com/index.php

You can also check any good sporting equipment store. When you order accessories, be sure to compare prices, keeping in mind that when you order online you will incur shipping charges. If you have a local Sports Authority, Dick's Sporting Goods, or similar store, you can make some purchases there.

Trendy Accessories

There are so many new accessories out in the market today that you will surely want to get yourself familiar with some of them (if you are not already). Using the newest accessories in your clients' workouts is a great benefit toward your reputation. It shows versatility and creativeness. Plus, it gives you more options for creating exciting and innovative workouts.

I will cover basic accessories in the next chapter, when I help you put together a list of equipment to purchase. Here I just want to encourage you to always keep abreast of the latest trends in exercise accessories. For example, right now kettlebells or Russian kettlebells are very popular. But this may not be the case as you are reading this. Maybe right now there is a new trend that doesn't even exist as I write this! That's why you have to keep up with the latest workout trends—and I am not talking about fads or fad diets, but real workouts that really work!

There are many places, including magazines and Web sites, where you can find and read up on the newest and latest exercise trends, such as:

- Shape.com
- Fitnesshealthzone.com
- *Women's Health*
- *Men's Health*
- *Shape*
- *Fitness*
- *Self*

Even watching the E! channel can keep you in the loop, as it often has stories about celebrities and the latest exercises they're doing to stay in Hollywood shape!

Scoping Out Your Competition

As you plan your new business, you will want to check to see if there is already a home-based personal trainer on every corner or if there is a lack of home-based personal trainers in your area. It's important to know if your market is saturated with your service or not.

If you find there is a dire need for personal trainers, kudos to you! The pro here is that you do not have much competition. The con is that you may be at a geographic disadvantage if your town is not much into health and fitness. You will just have to make an impact on the people around you and get them excited about getting fit.

On the other hand, you might find that your town *is* saturated with personal trainers. If this is the case, there's no need to worry. Keep on reading and keep your spirits high! Most of the personal trainers out there are probably handling their business half-heartedly. You are one up on them already by reading this book. If you apply what you learn and start your business full throttle, you can't lose! Plus a plethora of personal trainers in your area most likely means that the local population has a sizeable interest in hiring personal trainers to help them get in shape.

How to Scope Out the Competition

To find out about your competition, begin with a search on the Internet. Type in the phrase "personal trainers" and then the name of your town. You can also look in the yellow pages. Then go to the local gyms, find out how many trainers they have, and ask them if they also train out of their home.

If you live in a small town, it will be much easier to scope out the competition. In small towns it is easy to find information on people. Just speaking to your friends and acquaintances will give you a pretty good idea of how much competition you have.

If you live in a big city, it won't be as easy. But then again, you have a much larger population to target. It is also more likely that the personal trainers will be listed in the yellow pages and on the Internet.

Your Studio, and Why a "Studio"

This may seem insignificant, but it's not. When speaking to people about your business, you need to articulate in a way that sounds professional and convincing—convincing that your business is real and not just a romper room. And I think using the word *studio* will help you do just that. After all, would you rather tell people, "I will train you out of my home workout facility," "I can train you at my home gym," or "I can train you at my studio"? Doesn't the latter sound best?

The word *studio* gives your business a professional and real quality. It also gives you consistency, because you don't use a different word each time you refer to your business.

I am not saying that *studio* should be the *name* of your business; you should come up with a creative name that is all your own. I just mean you should use the word *studio* in conversation about your business.

03

What You Need in Your Home Office and Studio

Your Work Space

You will need an office or at least an office space for your home-based business. Here is where you will do your bookkeeping and marketing and create and manage your client files.

If your studio is large enough, you can carve out a corner for your office space. If you do this, you will have to be extra careful about keeping it neat and organized, as your clients will see. If your studio is only big enough to fit your equipment, and there is no room for an office space, then you need to find a spot in your home where you can fit a dedicated office space.

Furniture: Practical and Space-Saving

When you think about outfitting your office, think practical. Practical means an office that is both functional and efficient. You might be thinking you'll get one of those large ornate desks you see on television shows and expensive art for the walls, with sculptures and . . . okay, wake up! If you like to "go big" in everything you buy, the thought of furnishing your own office (if this is the first time) may make your thoughts run rampant. Most of you won't think this way, but this is why I feel it is necessary to include information on the essentials you will need for your home office.

Based on the square footage you can dedicate to your office space, you will need to incorporate different space-saving techniques. There are many ways to be creative in small spaces. One way is to use a corner desk, which usually provides a larger work surface while taking up less space. You can also get a desk with file cabinets underneath—either they fit underneath or the drawers are file cabinets. You can install shelves on the wall or use tall but not very wide bookcases for reference books. A tall bookcase is a great idea for using the wall space vertically, instead of using up a lot of useful horizontal space. If you get a tall bookcase, secure it to the wall to prevent it from tipping over.

Make Your Work Space Work for You

Not only do I want you to think about space and functionality, but you also need to think about what your personality deserves and demands from your office space. Are you a very organized person? Are you disorganized and/or do you create clutter? These are things to think about.

You should be happy with the setup of your studio and office space. In fact, both should be inspirational to you! To accomplish this, you need to dive into your own head to find out what will get you enthusiastic and energized to get your work done and make you want to get your work done. You may only be thinking about the personal training aspect of your business. But you will be sitting at your desk a few, sometimes many, hours a week. So your office space is just as important.

If your office is in a dreary corner of the basement, are you going to want to sit down there, or will you avoid it at all costs? Your business's success will rely partly on you doing your advertising, paying bills, and following up with clients. So avoiding your office will be detrimental to your business. If the dreary corner is the only possible place, that is okay. Just spiff it up to your standards. Put on your overalls and that old painter's hat and paint the space your favorite color and buy some posters to hang on the walls (inspirational or energetic posters usually work well). Also, make sure you have substantial lighting.

Where to Find Ideas to Create and Decorate Your Office

Create a Home Office: www.createhomeoffice.com

Decorate a Room: www.decorate-a-room.com/home-office.html

Better Homes and Gardens: www.bhg.com/decorating/room/home-office

How Stuff Works: http://home.howstuffworks.com/how-to-create-a-home-office.htm

All Posters: www.allposters.com

Office Furniture

There are several key pieces of furniture you will need for your office. Purchasing the right size furniture for your space is key. Be sure to measure your space prior to making purchases.

Here are the basics:

- Desk. Your desk will be the focal point of your office. There are many different types of desks: corner, hutch, roll-top, computer, L-shaped.
- Desk chair. It is a good idea to get an ergonomic chair, which will keep your spine aligned and pain away. An adjustable-height chair is a good alternative.
- Filing cabinet. You will need a filing cabinet for your client files, bookkeeping/ bills, and references (information you might print from your computer and/ or newspaper/magazine articles and client handouts). Keeping a neat and labeled file for these items will make your life a lot easier—or at least it will save you some time in the long run when you need to find something.
- Bookcase/shelves. Being your own boss, running your own business out of your home, you will most likely accumulate a library of books for reference and learning tools (starting with this one!). A bookcase or shelves is a great way to display your books for easy access.

Where to Research and Shop for Office Furniture

Start by visiting your local OfficeMax, Office Depot, or Staples. Then try the following Web sites:

Simply Desks: www.simplydesks.com

Ergonomic Chairs: www.ergonomicofficechairs.com

Beyond the Office Door: www.beyondtheofficedoor.com

Office Depot: www.officedepot.com

OfficeMax: www.officemax.com

Staples: www.Staples.com

FilingCabinets.com: www.filingcabinets.com

Home Decorators Collection: www.homedecorators.com

Office Equipment

Your office equipment—meaning electronics—is something that you should do a little, if not a lot, of research on before you buy. If you are experienced with this sort of technology and already know what works for you, then by all means just go out and shop!

Computer

Perhaps you already have a computer at home (now that we are in the twenty-first century, there is a good chance you do have a computer, maybe even two). If you share a computer with your family and/or spouse, you should get a separate computer for your office. It does not have to be anything fancy for this business, just a good basic desktop or laptop computer. Get the type you are familiar with, whether that is a PC (such as a Dell, IBM, Gateway, HP, and so on) or a Mac.

Software

You will need Microsoft Word to create documents and Excel to create and maintain spreadsheets and forms. You will also need a money-management software such as Quickbooks or MS Money.

For keeping a database of your clients, Filemaker Pro is used by many small businesses because it is easy to customize. Microsoft Access is another program that larger businesses use. It does a lot more, but it is more complex to set up. Filemaker is easier for do-it-yourselfers. An interesting fact is that Quickbooks can be used to keep track of your contacts in addition to your finances.

If you are experienced or plan to learn to be savvy with creating your own advertising and marketing materials, you might want to get a layout program, either QuarkXpress or inDesign; a photo-editing program such as Photoshop; and an illustration program such as Illustrator.

Back Up Your Work

If you overlook backing up your work, you will be in big trouble! You may already be a person who backs up his or her computer on a regular basis. However, if you have not already been doing this for your job or personal files, or if you have not had any reason to, now is a good time to drill into your head that you must back up your computer often—if not every day.

Choosing a Backup Device

I am not an expert on this topic, as you can tell by my horror story. So I went to the person who saves me when I have a computer problem and who taught me how to back up our files. Ronald Riccio, a computer technician in Kihei, Maui, has given me a wealth of information to share with you.

In the event your hardware fails or your security is breached, a data backup is your only hope of staying in business with no loss of time or money. *Always back up critical data daily!* There are too many threats to ignore this basic need, but unfortunately the vast majority of businesses have no regular data backup procedure in place. Human nature being what it is, *the backup must be automatic or it won't get done!* Don't trust good intentions; have a computer technician install an automated system and do regular checks of your backups to ensure the system is working properly.

Ideally you should have two backups: one physical copy stored locally and a second copy stored on a web-based data-storage service. The local copy can be put on a secondary internal or external hard drive, thumb drive (USB flash drive), or record-able CD or DVD. All of these options are better than no backup at all, but each has its advantages and disadvantages. An internal hard drive with automated backup software is the most foolproof, but it is vulnerable to the physical threats mentioned earlier. An external hard drive with automated software allows you to remove the drive from the premises nightly to prevent physical threats from destroying your backup. External hard drives come in two forms: self-powered 2.5-inch drives (which use laptop hard drives) and larger 3.5-inch drives (which use desktop hard drives and require an external AC adapter). The smaller hard drives are more convenient and portable, but they are less reliable and have shorter average life spans than the larger hard drives. Flash drives are very popular and convenient, but they have much smaller capacities and are easily lost. Recordable CDs and DVDs are a low-cost alter-native but require too much user interaction to be convenient or regularly used, and they have even smaller capacities than flash drives.

Web-based data storage services provide safe offsite storage that is invulnerable to attacks. The cost ranges from free (for up to five gigabytes of storage) to $50 to $100 per year and up for very large amounts of storage. The services provide soft-ware that automates the backup process and password protects the data. In most cases the data are available from any computer, allowing the user to access data from anywhere. This is a great complement to your local backup or it can be used as your only backup, if necessary. Having two separate data backups is best, however.

Data Security
Ronald Riccio also shares his knowledge of data security:

As a small business grows, it becomes more and more dependent on computers for maintaining its data, including billing and finances. Ironically, as this dependence and subsequent vulnerability grows, the attention paid to data security usually does not. We are either too busy or convinced that it won't happen to us. So we as small business owners go on pouring our life's blood into our business with a system that will inevitably fail at some point. It is critically important that you protect your data at all times.

The threats to your data take on two forms: internal mechanical failure and an external attack of some form. Internal failures include anything that physically threatens the hard drive, including crashes due to age or misuse, power supply surges and spikes, physical damage (such as fire, water, dropping, or impact), and overheating. Protect your computer by keeping it in a safe, room-temperature area where the air vents and fans are clean. Use a good-quality surge suppressor to prevent AC-power fluctuations from blowing the power supply and internal components. An even better solution is an uninterruptable battery backup system (UPS), which has better line-voltage stabilization and can keep the computer running for a short period during a power outage. This allows the user to complete the current operation and perform an orderly system shutdown (preventing a hard drive crash and data loss). Some UPS units can do the shutdown unattended.

The second threat is from external sources: hackers, viruses, spyware, corrupted data, user error, sabotage (disgruntled former employees frequently take out their frustration on the computers), and theft. At a minimum your computer should have antivirus, antispyware, and firewall software installed. However, even when protective measures to prevent outside attacks are in place, you must monitor and maintain these defenses. If the particular defense program doesn't run automatically in the background, make sure to update it and manually run complete scans at least once a week.

The most critical defense is the antivirus program. *It must be running at all times when the system is turned on.* There are cases where a minor glitch can cause Windows Explorer (the desktop) to do a minor self-reboot. You can tell if this has happened by looking at the icons in the "tool tray" (lower right-hand corner of the desktop). If any of the normal icons are missing (especially the antivirus icon), *do not*

What Not to Do

- Do not load any software, data, or photos from personal disks or thumb drives unless you run an antivirus scan first. The risk to critical company data is just too great.

- Do not open e-mail or attachments from unknown sources or from known sources if the e-mail comes unexpected or lacks a personal message in its body. Viruses spread by mailing themselves from infected machines that you may recognize as "friends" but that your friend didn't actually send. It's also possible that a friend does not know he or she has and is spreading a virus. If you get an unexpected e-mail from a friend, e-mail or call your friend to make sure he or she intended to send it to you.

continue to use the computer. Reboot the computer, which will force the system to reload the background programs.

Spyware has surpassed viruses as the main system attack problem. It gets into the system through corrupted Web sites you visit, devious fine print agreements you "accept" when signing up for login data, and in e-mails and attachments. It causes system slowdowns by constantly gathering information about the user and sending it back to the marketing company of origin. At its worst it can acquire private data, passwords, and financial data and constitute a major security breach.

Printer

You will need a decent printer to print forms, waivers, and workout charts. A good place to start looking for one is your local office supply store. You will probably find several printers in the $125 to $300 range. I suggest you get an all-in-one printer that prints, faxes, scans, and copies. These are often called "four-in-one" printers. They not only save you money, but they also save space.

Opt for a higher-end printer if you plan on creating and printing your own fliers, business cards, brochures, or any other advertising materials. You may spend more on the printer, but if you are able to create and print some of your own marketing materials, you will save a bundle on graphic designers and printing.

Fax Machine

Faxing is not as popular as it once was, but it is still useful and a good option to have. If you have your fax machine included in your printer, then you will be all set. You should not need a separate fax line; hooking it up to your office phone should be good enough for the little you will use it.

There are also online fax services such as efax.com and myfax.com. Basically, when you receive a fax it comes to you in an e-mail attachment. The monthly cost for this service is approximately $10 to $17. You can also send faxes with these services through your computer. This may not be the most economical choice, depending on how often you use the fax, but if you prefer to do everything online, this may be a convenient option for you.

Phones: Cell Phone, Land Line, or Both

As with everything else in today's world, phone technology seems to change every day. For personal use and your one-person home business, a cell phone may be all you need. If you are a traditionalist, or if you want your business line to be as professional as possible, you may prefer a land line.

A cell phone is a good option if you are prepared to have a phone dedicated to your business. Your voicemail should be professional and state that this is your business line. Most cell phone companies have plans that enable you to add a second line for as little as $10 extra per month.

A cell phone is portable and can be with you most of the time. However, this can be both a good and a bad thing—depending on how you look at it. It's good that your clients will never have to wait very long for you to return their calls. What's more, a potential new client will see that you get back to them quickly. On the other hand, your clients may call while you are in the middle of a romantic dinner or while you are reading a bedtime story to your child. This happens often nowadays, as most people have their cell phone on them all the time. One way around this is to get a second cell phone that would be strictly for your business. This way you can leave the phone in your office during times you need a break, but still have it with you the majority of the time to give your clients the best possible service.

Office Supplies

You will need plenty of supplies in your office. The following supplies will make getting and staying organized easy:

- Stapler and staples
- Scissors
- Scotch tape
- Paper clips
- Pens
- Pencils
- Binder clips
- Bulletin board
- Push pins
- Three-hole punch
- File folders
- Printer/copy paper
- Printer ink
- Highlighters

- Post-it note pads
- Letter-size envelopes (#10)
- Desk or wall calendar
- Rubber bands

Safety Equipment and Tools

Your home-based business stands apart from most home-based businesses in that you not only will have people entering your home, but they will be engaging in physical activity. You have to be prepared for an emergency; you never know when someone might get injured, or worse, collapse. I don't mean to scare you, but this is the reality when you are in this business. If you are an experienced trainer, chances are you may have been in the gym when an ambulance had to be called or when someone passed out while exerting too much energy. If you are a newbie, then you should carefully read the following information.

Defibrillator

When you suspect someone is in cardiac arrest, *call 911 first*. Then, as you wait for help to arrive, you can use a defibrillator. A defibrillator is an electronic device that sends an electric shock to the heart to stop an extremely rapid, irregular heartbeat and restore the normal heart rhythm.

American AED (Automated External Defibrillators) is perhaps the most popular company that sells defibrillators. You can find their Web site at www.americanaed .com. These devices are not inexpensive—at approximately $1,200, this is a steep purchase—but it a wise investment and could save a life.

First Aid Kit

You should *always* have a first aid kit in your studio. You can purchase first aid supplies at stores such as Wal-Mart, Target, or K-Mart. You can purchase an already assembled kit, or you can put one together yourself. Either way, make sure it has all the necessary items, which according to the American Red Cross includes the following:

- Absorbent compress dressings (5x9 inches)
- Adhesive bandages (assorted sizes)
- 1-inch-wide adhesive cloth tape (10 yards)

- 5 antibiotic ointment packets (approximately 1 gram)
- 5 antiseptic wipe packets
- 1 blanket (space blanket)
- 1 breathing barrier (with one-way valve)
- 1 instant cold compress
- 2 pair nonlatex gloves (large)
- 2 hydrocortisone ointment packets
- Scissors
- 1 roller bandage (3 inches wide)
- 1 roller bandage (4 inches wide)
- 5 sterile gauze pads (3x3 inches)
- 5 sterile gauze pads (4x4 inches)
- 2 triangular bandages
- Tweezers
- First aid instruction booklet

Make sure your first aid kit is always well stocked. Don't wait until you have completely run out of adhesive bandages, for example, before you replenish the supply.

In addition to having a first aid kit, you should be trained in handling emergencies. For information on training and certification for first aid, CPR, and defibrillators, see chapter 13.

Materials Needed to Create Your Studio

You have chosen a space for your studio and have thought about the layout. You have also thought about how to make your studio visually inviting and comfortable. In this section I will cover the materials you will use to cover or dress your studio.

Flooring/Mats

There are several options to choose from when deciding on your floor. I am a big fan of rubber flooring. Rubber not only offers cushion and resiliency and is easy to clean (making it much easier to keep disinfected), it also is an easy way to add color and liveliness to your studio for a not-so-high price tag! Your best bet is interlocking rubber blocks. They range in size from twelve-inch to forty-eight-inch squares. The twenty-four-inch squares are a happy medium. With rubber tiles you can mix and match colors to make your studio fun and bright, or you can go with all one color. An additional benefit is that if one tile rips or gets stained, you can easily replace the one tile with minimal cost. Plus, rubber is a great protective barrier for the floor beneath.

If for some reason I have not sold you on rubber tiles, you can opt for carpet. You should get the carpet professionally cleaned often, or to save money in the long run, invest in a steam cleaner. Carpet can be nice, but it can harbor dirt, germs, and odors.

Mirrors

Mirrors are key when working out. They help you to keep your form in check and allow you to smile (or frown) at your progress in becoming fit and tone.

Mirrors do not need to cover every inch of your wall space, but you should have at least some mirrors. A good place for mirrors is where your clients will be using dumbbells, fit balls, or other core/balancing equipment.

To find mirrors, look in your local yellow pages under the word *glass*, or search online for mirrors. Mirrors can be costly, so you may want to search Craig's List (www .craigslist.org), where you might find used mirrors.

When installing mirrors, it is imperative to make sure they are secured safely to the wall. The last thing you want is for a mirror to come crashing down in the middle of a training session. You might even consider purchasing shatterproof mirrors. There is a glue made specifically for hanging mirrors; you can find it at Lowe's or Home Depot. It's also a good idea to secure a long piece of wood under the bottom edge of the mirrors. This will give them added support.

Music

You will probably want music playing in the background as you train and work. You can probably use a device you already own. An iPod with speakers is a good option, as is a CD player. It is not necessary to go out and get an expensive sound system. However, what you don't want to do is play the radio. No one wants to hear commercials or the weather update while working out.

Major Equipment Purchases

You should put a lot of thought into your equipment purchases. After all, these are major decisions that can affect your business and profitability. The purchase of your equipment should be based on three things: money, your training style, and your space.

Budget

How much you have to spend on equipment will have a great impact on what you can buy. Will you purchase commercial or residential equipment? Will it be new or refurbished/remanufactured?

Your Training Style

Your training style will impact your equipment purchases. In this book, I will give you just a basic blueprint of what you will need to get started; this is not cast in stone. The ultimate decisions will be up to you. I will simply suggest what you will need in order to train a variety of clients as you begin your business to help you capture more revenue.

Your Space

The amount of space you have will determine how much equipment you will be able to fit into your studio. I recommend a minimum of 300 square feet. But in addition to the amount of space you have, the dimensions of your studio are also important. If you have a 20-foot by 12-foot room, that is only 240 square feet. But the room may be long enough to place equipment along the wall while still leaving you with a nice-size area to train clients. This would work just fine. Also bear in mind that your ceiling height will play a part in determining what equipment will fit as well.

Refurbished Equipment

Refurbished, or remanufactured, equipment is a great way to get commercial equipment at roughly half the price. Most remanufactured equipment today is only a few years old. That's because there is a constant rush of new products to market that highlight advancements in product design, ranging from built-in LCD televisions to electronic advancements that include network affiliations and electronic personal trainers. In order to keep a competitive edge, gym owners need to stay one step ahead or at least keep up with their competitors. So they keep buying the latest and greatest equipment.

In order to keep up, the larger gyms sell their old (or really only slightly used) equipment to companies that specialize in refurbishing and selling used fitness equipment. These companies bid on a gym's equipment and get it for pennies on the dollar. They then rebuild it—replacing parts and repainting the frames—and then resell it. When they are done refurbishing the equipment—whether it is a treadmill, elliptical, or piece of strength-training equipment—the average personal training client would never be able to tell that the equipment was refurbished.

All refurbished equipment is vigorously tested by certified specialists to ensure performance. But for peace of mind, the companies that sell refurbished equipment

Companies That Sell Refurbished Equipment

There are many companies that deal in refurbished and remanufactured equipment. Here are a few:

Global Fitness, founded in 1992, is a multinational corporation based in Los Angeles. Its 105,000-square-foot facility is the largest of its kind in the world. They also have a 20,000-square-foot facility in Rotterdam, Netherlands, and a large warehouse and distribution facility in Ontario, Canada. Global Fitness works with all the top equipment manufacturers in the United States, including Life Fitness, Precor, Star Trac, Cybex, Nautilus, and many more. Working with so many companies ensures that they have a consistent flow of products. Global Fitness's warranty on cardiovascular equipment is six months on parts and labor and one year on motors. They also sell extended warranties and state that if anyone can beat their prices in an apple-to-apple comparison, they will match the price and offer a further 5 percent discount. Call Global Fitness at (888) 991-9991.

USA Fitness Direct is based out of California, with facilities in Utah and Texas. They deal in brands such as Life Fitness, Precor, Star Trac, Stairmaster, Cybex, Bodymasters, and more. Most equipment comes with a six-month warranty on parts and labor and one year on motors. A seven- to ten-year warranty is offered on most strength equipment, with a one-year warranty on moving parts. They also state that they offer lease programs. USA Fitness Direct can be reached at (866) 487-2348.

GoodFitness.com is located in Southern California and deals in brands such as Life Fitness, Star Trac, Precor, Nautilus, and more. They also have their own line of strength equipment. The company sells a full line of accessories such as balance tools, bars, attachments, stability balls, flooring/mats, nutritional supplements, and more. Call GoodFitness.com at (800) 657-4348.

offer warranties on their equipment. The standard warranty on cardio equipment such as a treadmill or elliptical is a full six months, with one year on the drive motor/ alternator. The standard warranty on strength equipment is five to ten years on the frame and one year on the moving parts. Any new upholstery is under warranty from the material manufacturer.

Overall, buying refurbished equipment is a great way to get commercial equipment at a great price and to impress your clients.

Commercial or Residential Equipment?

The difference in cost between residential and commercial equipment is substantial. If it is within your budget to purchase new commercial equipment, that is ideal. However, many people just starting out simply cannot afford it.

I suggest purchasing residential equipment only if it is from one of the large brand names like Precor, Star Trac, Life Fitness, or Nautilus, which in most cases will cost as much as a piece of refurbished commercial equipment. If you have to choose between these two options, go for the refurbished commercial equipment.

Residential equipment will look cheap to your clients. Imagine walking into your local gym to join. You pay your enrollment fee and go over to the treadmill. When you get there, you see that you could have bought the same treadmill at Sears for the cost of your club membership. Or suppose you did not yet join the gym and are being given a tour by the sales representative. Along the way you see that the equipment is designed for home use. What are the chances that you would join?

Remember that image means a whole lot in the fitness industry. How you present yourself, how you dress, and, yes, how your fitness studio looks are all elements of image that add up to helping you achieve success—or not.

Cardio Equipment

Now it's time to think about the actual pieces of equipment you will purchase. After speaking with several personal trainers and from my own experience in this business, the one piece of cardio equipment that you have to have is a treadmill. Why? Because it is very simple for clients to warm up on a treadmill. Approximately 70 percent of trainers' clients warm up on a treadmill for ten to fifteen minutes, mostly walking at a brisk pace. Treadmills require very little skill or coordination to use. You can easily monitor your clients' time, and as they gain fitness you can easily up their speed and incline.

Cardio Choices

These are my top picks for cardio equipment:

- Treadmills offer a variety of options, including walking, speed walking, jogging, and running. Opt for a treadmill with the incline option for more versatility. This can be a low-impact workout if you walk.

- Ellipticals provide an excellent cardiovascular workout with very low impact.

- Stationary bikes provide a low-impact cardio workout and are efficient in their use of space.

- Stairmasters or steppers work the legs and glutes, offer a good cardio workout, and may increase balance. The downside is that stepping is a weight-bearing exercise, so this workout may cause or increase injury in the knees and/or hips.

After getting a treadmill, if it is within your budget and space, it would be great to get a second piece of cardio equipment. If this is the case, I suggest an elliptical machine. Elliptical machines are a great choice because they provide an excellent cardiovascular workout, work both the upper and lower body, and are very low-impact. This is important for people who are injury prone, recovering from an injury, or elderly. Low impact means that there is very little chance of injury to the back, knees, or other joints.

Strength Equipment

For strength equipment I highly recommend that you invest in a functional trainer. This is a great piece of equipment to have because of the wide variety of exercises you can perform on it. From chest exercises to legs, biceps, triceps, and much more, this equipment ensures that your clients never get bored with their workouts and helps them achieve results. Also, as you would imagine, a functional trainer is many pieces in one, saving both space and money! Many large, reputable companies manufacture functional trainers. It is up to you to decide which one suits you best. No matter which one you choose, a functional trainer will be a great choice and is bound to help your clients get results.

> **Top Picks for a Functional Trainer**
>
> FreeMotion Fitness makes my favorite functional trainer, called the FreeMotion EXT Dual Cable Cross. This is their light-commercial functional trainer. Each arm rotates vertically in twelve settings and horizontally in nine settings to accommodate any movement. It sells for approximately $4,000, while the commercial one, called the FreeMotion Dual Cable Cross, sells for approximately $6,000.
>
> Precor makes a residential functional trainer that in my opinion looks just like a commercial one. It's called the FTS (Functional Training System), is part of Precor's Icarian Strength line, and sells for approximately $6,000.
>
> Keiser makes a good functional trainer, too. I like this one because its design is more compact than most others, and its two adjustable arms not only make it easy to store but allow you to do many additional exercises for high or low training positions. This functional trainer sells for approximately $4,000.

Strength Equipment Attachments and Accessories

There are several attachments you will need for your functional trainer: cable attachments, straps, and ropes. All of the companies that sell functional trainers sell the accessory kits, and most if not all will give these attachments to you for free with your purchase of the functional trainer—if you negotiate it right. And this could be a great savings, as some of these attachments can cost $40. The entire attachment/accessory kit can range between $180 and $400.

If you need attachments or additional attachments along the way, most sporting goods stores sell them.

Additional Strength Equipment

Listed here are some other strength-training pieces you might want to consider.

Weight Bench

Whether working out with dumbbells or your functional trainer, this is a must-have for any fitness facility. The best thing you can do is get an adjustable bench. Prices range from $450 to $750.

Dumbbells

Dumbbells are another must-have for your studio, but they can become a big expense. For example, one 10-pound dumbbell can run from $15 all the way up to $45—for a single dumbbell! With the cost increasing as the weight increases, this can certainly add up.

There is a way to keep the cost of dumbbells down and save space, however. And that's by purchasing adjustable dumbbells, also known as interchangeable dumbbells. Most standard adjustable dumbbells range from 5 pounds to 50 pounds. Some brands allow you to adjust the weight in 2.5- to 5-pound increments. The price of a pair of adjustable dumbbells ranges from $350 to $450 for the top brands. If you go with adjustable dumbbells, you will also need to get the stand (rack) for the weights, which is approximately $150. This is still a good deal, though, because if you purchased a set of individual dumbbells of all different weights, you would most likely want a rack for them, which would run you around $300. With that in mind, getting adjustable dumbbells will save you approximately $600 to $700.

One downside to keep in mind as you decide which dumbbells to purchase is that the adjustable dumbbells can be time-consuming. If you are unable to change the weight quickly in between sets, this can get frustrating and waste valuable time for you and your clients.

Essential Exercise Accessories

In this section I will give you an overview of the small, or less costly, exercise accessories I suggest you purchase for your studio. I like to refer to these items as the "fun accessories." My suggestions are based on what I have found to be popular and the most functional accessories. Of course it is not possible to list every accessory that exists; there are just too many choices.

Some popular accessories, the ones I believe your studio should have, include the following:

- BOSU Balance Trainer
- Medicine balls (three or four different weights, ranging between four and twelve pounds)
- Fit balls (three or four sizes: 45 cm, 55 cm, 65 cm, 75 cm); I also highly recommend getting a stability ball wall storage rack. (Power-Systems sells one for about $70.) This rack is easy to hang on your wall and keeps the balls off the floor when they're not in use.
- Resistance bands or tubing; good for both stretching and resistance strength training, resistance bands and tubing are multifunctional, cost very little, and take up hardly any space at all.

You should also have at least two mats (such as yoga mats) for floor exercises. Having two mats is good so you can use one while demonstrating an exercise.

You do not have to get all of your accessories at once. You can start out with the basics and add more as your cash flow increases.

Optional Accessories to Add Diversity

If you are an experienced trainer, you may already know about all of these accessories, or if you are new to the business, you may be an avid gym rat who also knows about them. Possibly you are new to the world of gyms and fancy accessories. Whatever your situation, you will have so much to think about when starting your business that your brain might go into overload. So to help you out, here are some fun accessories that you may overlook that can jazz up your studio and training sessions.

As I mentioned before, there is always a trendy new exercise accessory on the market. But you need not go out and buy every accessory that comes out; that would be unrealistic and unnecessary. It is a good idea, however, to keep your eyes open for new trends and then pick and choose those you want to learn to use for training your clients. Here are some of those:

- *Kettlebells.* Some of the benefits of kettlebells are fat loss, increased endurance, and increased muscle mass. The prices start at approximately $30 for a ten-pound kettlebell.
- *Yoga blocks.* These are used for extra balance and support during poses. Prices start at approximately $10.
- *Yoga/Pilates core bands.* These bands create greater articulation of the body's core movements, enhancing strength. Prices start at approximately $25.

- *Foam rollers.* These accessories develop balance, postural alignment, and flexibility. They can also be used as a support for strength exercises. Prices start at approximately $9.
- *Kickboxing gloves and shield.* Use these to help build upper-body strength and coordination. Gloves start at $20 per pair; a forearm shield starts at approximately $25.
- *Rocker and wobble boards.* These help improve balance and posture and increase core strength. Prices start at approximately $30.

These are just the tip of the iceberg when it comes to accessories, but they are certainly a good start for diversity and to bring some well-rounded choices to your studio.

Testing Accessories

You will likely do some sort of evaluation when you first meet with a new client. This may include performing body-fat tests, taking body measurements, and measuring weight. Also, over time, you and your clients will want to track their progress using one or more forms of testing. Here are a few testing items you may use:

- *Body fat calipers* measure body fat by measuring a fold of skin. If you use this tool, make sure you have researched how to use it as effectively as possible. There is a lot of room for error with this tool.
- *Body fat analyzers* are handheld devices that display body fat percentage and body mass index (BMI).
- *Body tape measure* helps you measure and keep track of body measurements.

Real-Life Story

Certified personal trainer Alicia Adkins of Kihei, Maui, had a client who did not want to get on a scale, have her body fat measured, or do any other test that would put numbers or facts to her weight. So Alicia got creative and asked her client to bring in a pair of pants—a pair that fit her at her current fitness level. Every two weeks, her client brought the same pair of pants in to her session. This was a very effective—and creative—way to measure her progress.

- *Scales* keep track of weight loss/gain.
- *Heart rate monitors* help you to regulate workout intensity and make sure clients are within a safe heart rate range.

Think Outside the Box

You will not be able to treat each client in the same way. Each will have a different personality—some shy, some self-conscious, some very confident, some not so confident. What's more, each client will have different goals. Some will want weight loss, while others will want to build muscle tone; some will want to gain weight, while still others will simply want to improve their health and quality of life.

Taking all of this into consideration, you will have to be creative when it comes to evaluating your clients or tracking their progress. If you suggest a body fat analysis to a client, and he or she does not want to do that, do not insist or try to talk him or her into it. Later on as your client progresses, he or she may be secure enough to take the test. In the meantime, tailor your evaluation with techniques that will make your client feel comfortable and might even be fun for him or her. All along you will be building trust between you and your client. If you want to track progress, you could just have your client look in the mirror to see the changes. Or you could take before and after pictures; maybe even take a new picture each month to monitor progress (have your client wear the same outfit in each picture).

Disinfecting and Cleaning Supplies

Another aspect imperative to your success, your reputation, and the safety of your studio is keeping a healthy environment. After each client you should clean the equipment he or she used. Simply use a spray bottle with a combination of bleach and water or a commercial cleaning solution.

Where to Purchase Accessories and Testing Equipment

Power-Systems: www.power-systems.com
Club Purchasing Service: www.club-supplies.com
Yoga Direct: www.yogadirect.com
Healthy Styles Exercise Equipment: www.healthystylesexercise.com

Keep It Clean

Among the top reasons you might lose clients is cleanliness. If your studio is dirty or even just messy, you *will* lose clients. Maintaining a clean studio is one of the easiest ways to keep clients. And cleaning your studio does not have to take much time, as long as you keep up with it every day.

Owning a ten-thousand-square-foot gym, I know all about how difficult it is to keep a workout facility clean! However, your studio is much smaller, and you will have only one (maybe two) people working out at a time. You will endure much less wear and tear, much less dripping sweat, much less dirt all around. However, you are also just one person, so keeping up with it is solely your responsibility.

Real-Life Story

Not mentioning any names . . . but I have seen firsthand what happens when a workout facility gets run down and dirty. When I co-owned and operated a gym, our main competition was a run-down facility that reaped many complaints. Members from this facility would come into my gym and be so surprised and so appreciative that it was kept clean and that the equipment was all working properly. If something did break, we would fix it immediately or as quickly as possible.

The competition lost a large number of members to our newer, cleaner facility. This was bound to happen. Who wants to work out where the weights are peeling, the floors are filthy, the restrooms are unkempt, and the treadmills don't work?

Workout facilities, no matter how large or how small, are breeding grounds for germs and bacteria (and even disease—hepatitis is a concern) to grow. Do your job: Make it a top priority to keep your studio as clean and disinfected as possible—not only for the health and safety of your clients, but for yourself!

In addition to cleaning the equipment after each use, mop the floor every day. Also, disinfect your accessories (such as fit balls and medicine balls) as often as necessary, most likely twice a week.

Here is a list of cleaning supplies you will need:

- Spray bottle(s)
- Bleach
- Commercial cleaning solution
- Rags
- Mop and bucket
- Window cleaner (for mirrors)
- Antibacterial spray (for doorknobs and other surfaces)

04

Writing a Business Plan

Purpose of a Business Plan

If the thought of writing a business plan makes you want to jump off the closest bridge, you are not alone. Writing a business plan can be scary, because it is an adventure into the unknown. However, it is like most everything else: Once you understand it and why it is important, and once you get started, it is not that scary after all!

Writing a business plan is an important step in the process of starting your home-based business for several reasons. One reason is that if you are applying for a loan, especially a small business loan (SBA loan), the bank will require a business plan. Another reason is that writing a business plan is similar to creating an outline for your business. It will enable you to see the big picture—from the beginning stages all the way through to the time when your business is established. As you write your business plan, you will be able to focus more clearly on exactly what your business will entail. It will help you prepare for each step of starting the business and help you to understand parts that may not be too clear to you in the beginning. Your business plan will be a statement of what your goals are, why they are reachable, and how you will attain these goals.

The feeling of accomplishment and your broader sense of understanding will be well worth the time and effort spent to write your business plan. Having a business plan will also make your business feel more important and real, making you want to give it 100 percent of your effort.

How to Get Started

If this is not your first business venture and you have written a business plan in the past, you can use that one as a template, changing the necessary information to fit your new plan. If you have never written a business plan, a good place to start is the Internet. However, *do not* buy an already written business plan; you will only be cheating yourself. Taking the easy way or lazy way out is not going to make a positive foundation for your new business. But there are many useful and helpful Web sites out there that can give you guidelines, including sample business plans and even templates, which will give you a good start.

Fundamentals of Your Business Plan

For the most part, all business plans are broken down into the same components. I will provide you with an example of each one from the business plan we created when Jerry and I opened our Powerhouse Gym. Granted, you will change it around to be conducive to your home-based fitness facility.

Executive Summary

Under this section, we used four subsections:

1. Introduction
2. Fitness Positioning
3. Market Considerations
4. The Competition

Here is an example of the Fitness Positioning subsection from our business plan:

Fitness Positioning

Powerhouse Fitness programs and services will focus on providing practical lifestyle enhancement to its members in an upbeat, friendly, yet sophisticated adult-oriented atmosphere. This serious but "non-threatening" approach to fitness and health will set it apart from other area facilities and provide the means to capture a larger share of our target market. As a first-class exercise facility, it will deliver the highest level of personal service and attention to its members. This approach contrasts sharply from other area facilities that include the traditional hard-core gyms, the impersonal low-cost/no-service environments, and the one-club-fits-all philosophy found in the traditional health and athletic clubs.

Your Business Plan

As a one-on-one personal training studio, your business plan may be more simple and not as in-depth as ours was. This is good news for you—less work!

When you create your business plan, focus on your service and your mission. Once you think about it, you already have the business plan in your head. Or you will by the time you finish this book.

Keep the formality of the business plan out of your mind and think about what you plan to offer your community.

Business Definition

Under this section I have five subsections:

1. Mission Statement
2. Legal Structure
3. Financial Requirements
4. Financial Breakdown of Start-up Costs
5. Feasibility Study Variables

Here is an example of the Mission Statement subsection.

Mission Statement

Powerhouse Gym fitness provides first-class comprehensive fitness and nutritional solutions designed to enhance its members' health and well-being. It does this in a friendly, non-intimidating atmosphere, which is focused on providing superior personal service and attention to detail.

Your Business Plan

You want to gear your mission statement to your goals and "mission," something along the lines of: "A personal training experience that will provide my clients with the utmost service and results. A one-on-one personal experience that will enhance my clients' overall well-being and health."

Phrase your mission statement however you want, in your own words—it is your vision. I am just giving you some insight.

Fitness Market

Under this section I have four subsections:

1. Industry Overview
2. Industry Trends
3. Geographic Area Map
4. Demographic Profile

Here is an example of the Industry Trends subsection:

Industry Trends

With government estimates suggesting that if people spent thirty minutes a day engaging in physical activity, it would save the United States more than $8 billion a year in health care and related costs, this has become the focus for much advertising and promotional activity, highlighting the benefits of exercise.

Like many lifestyle activities, health and fitness are affected by the vagaries of fashion trends. In the late 1980s, the market was dominated by the boom in aerobics, led by celebrities like Jane Fonda. During the 1990s, exercise became more intense, and innovations like the Reebok Step and boxercise—a cross between boxing and martial arts—were increasingly popular.

By the end of the 1990s, and reflecting changing lifestyle trends, more gentle forms of exercise such as yoga and Pilates were increasingly in demand.

In the new millennium, cardio kickboxing, Swiss-ball, and spin and body sculpting have become the most popular group exercise classes. Personal training revenues have soared in recent years and have become a major profit center.

It is paramount for owners to continue to recognize changes in the industry and to continue to accommodate their members. This is not limited to changing trends in group exercise. Owners must also continue to reinvest in their club's equipment, services, and amenities. This will assure long-term member retention.

Your Business Plan

The above is already outdated, as the trends are always changing—and rapidly. You can go as far back as you want with trends, but the 1980s are already old news—we are almost three decades out! Perhaps you can start with the 1990s or even the year 2000. Current trends may include (but are not limited to) boot camp–style exercise classes, plyometrics, and kettlebells. Exercise balls and core workouts are also very popular now. The overall well-being of one's mind and body is big now, as we approach the second decade of the twenty-first century. While working out was once about looking good, current trends show that more and more people work out to stay healthy and for spiritual well-being (bringing yoga into the mix).

Project Overview

Under this section I have five subsections:

1. What Is Powerhouse Gym?
2. Products and Services Offered
3. Business Strategies
4. Membership Types
5. Technology Position

Here is an example of the Products and Services Offered subsection:

Products and Services Offered

Through commitment to unsurpassed professional and personal service throughout all aspects of the facility, Powerhouse intends to propel itself into a prominent market position. Each staff member will be expertly trained in exercise programming and instruction, customer service, personal appearance, and facility cleanliness. The facility will offer state-of-the-art resistance and cardiovascular equipment, with the most advanced programming in the market as follows:

Aerobics: The aerobics program will be taught by insured professional instructors. There will be several aerobics classes per day, which will include beginner, intermediate, and advanced classes. The classes will be taught on a state-of-the-art suspended wood floor.

Personal Training: All trainers will be professionally certified and knowledgeable in the fields of fitness programming, nutrition, exercise physiology, and sports-specific training. The trainers will provide the first session free of charge to all members to encourage further participation in our structured personal training program.

Free Weights: The free-weight section will be the finest state-of-the-art quality available. Equipment will be provided by reputable manufacturers such as Icarian, Hammer Strength, and Cybex. The free-weight section of the facility will be utilized by all members including beginners, who will be supervised by our staff of professional trainers.

Circuit Training: The circuit-training program and equipment address full-body workouts for beginners and intermediates. The equipment is designed to be user-friendly and efficient to allow for maximum results in minimum time. The circuit-training program will appeal to those people with time constraints, such as business executives, homemakers, the nearby working population, and short-term visitors to the area.

Cardiovascular Equipment: The facility will have a diverse section of computerized cardiovascular equipment, including steppers, recumbent bikes, upright bikes, treadmills, and elliptical movement machines. This equipment appeals to clientele of all ages with varying degrees of ability and coordination. With multiples of each machine type, Powerhouse Gym will provide a complete inventory to adequately accommodate the membership's maximum use times.

Cardio Theater: Exercise entertainment has proven itself to be an invaluable tool in attracting and retaining members. Television/video monitors will be visible from all cardio equipment to help members "pass the time."

Pro Shop: At the end of a great workout, members can check out the pro shop, which will carry the latest in fashionable activewear, sportswear, and training aids for men and women. The pro shop will include a complete line of the hot-selling Powerhouse logo wear for before, during, and after member workouts. A full line of vitamins and supplements for any nutritional need will also be offered. The Powerhouse sportswear line will also be purchased by nonmembers as gifts, as souvenirs, and for personal use.

Child Care: A professionally designed and staffed child care area will be available for members to leave their children during their workouts. All child-care staff will be CPR and first aid certified.

Your Business Plan

Your products and services may be limited to just services, as most likely—in the beginning anyway—you will not be offering any products. Perhaps once you are open for a while and become established and comfortable with your services, you will begin to offer products (see chapter 12). Tailor this subsection of your business plan to whatever you will be offering.

You can always say that in the future (include an estimated time line) you will offer products such as supplements and nutrition counseling. Perhaps you can also say that you will eventually add elements such as boot camp–style group classes or yoga.

Strategy and Implementation

Under this section I have eight subsections:

1. Member Profile
2. Fitness Center Atmosphere
3. Presale Introduction and Overview
4. Pre-Opening/Presale Plan
5. Presale Office Lead Box Setup
6. Marketing Strategy
7. Inside Marketing
8. Web Site

Here is an example of the Fitness Center Atmosphere subsection:

Fitness Center Atmosphere

The Powerhouse Gym's atmosphere will be intentionally crafted to appeal to our target members. The goal will be to provide a feeling of community within the gym. The members will feel as if they are "coming home" when they are greeted by name. A great restaurant is judged not by its food alone, but also by its service and ambiance. We go back to our "favorite restaurant" again and again because it meets our expectations consistently. We become comfortable revisiting and look forward to the experience it provides.

Your Business Plan

You will formulate this section to *your* vision. Think about several questions:

- Who will your target clientele be? You may include one or more niches.
- What type of atmosphere will you be presenting? Will it be sophisticated and quiet or colorful and energetic? Remember: This is your dream, your vision.
- What marketing tools will you use prior to opening? This is your version of "presales."
- What will your Web site consist of? Will you include minimal information or a plethora of information? How creative will you get? (For more about Web sites, see chapter 11.)

Business Objectives and Goals

Under this section I have one subsection: Business/Financial Goals. Here is an example:

Business/Financial Goals

The following are the business objectives that the club has set as its goals:

- Facility construction and the opening of our presale office should commence within ninety days after the lease is signed. During the presale, memberships will be offered at a reduced rate and a grand opening will be promoted through the local media. There will be a full-scale model present at the presale.
- The goal in the first twelve months is to carry an active membership of approximately 1,200 members and to have a monthly receivable membership base of over $46,000 in membership dues.
- There will be a fully stocked pro shop, juice bar, and nutrition center by opening day.
- Staff will be fully trained to implement sales and programs by opening day.
- We will provide members with the best environment and the best of everything that is available in the fitness industry. This will apply to the facility, staff, equipment, merchandise, nutrition information, and supplements.
- We will maintain the equipment and facility in an impeccable manner.

- We will develop a sound public relations and community involvement campaign. The facility's public relations efforts will be directed at developing a network among sports institutions, media outlets, and community service organizations. It will serve as a source of fitness expertise for the community and will sponsor sporting events and local community teams. The club's employees will contact key people in sports, media, and community affairs and make them aware of the gym and fitness club and the special services it can provide.

Your Business Plan

Your objectives and goals section will focus more on the second portion of the objectives and goals listed above. You will not really have presales. In advance of opening, you should instead be marketing your business. More than likely you will not actually sell anything until you are open for business. You can write about how you will operate on a daily basis and keep up and maintain your facility. You may also include your anticipated involvement in the community and possible volunteer work you will do. You should also include how many clients you expect to have at opening and what your expected monthly receivables will be for your first twelve months in operation.

Organization and Staffing

Under this section I have two subsections:

1. The Management Team
2. Staffing Overview

Here is an example of the Management Team subsection:

The Management Team

Keep in mind that this was written more than six years ago.

Jerry Santarpia, General Manager/Owner

Mr. Santarpia has been in the carpentry/construction industry for eighteen years. He obtained experience as an apprentice and worked his way up to a journeyman carpenter. After several years he started his own carpentry company, specializing in kitchen and bath remodeling and complete renovations and extensions. Mr.

Santarpia was approached by Component Assembly Systems and offered a position as a foreman with their New York City office.

He supervised major projects including Reuter's Instinet World Headquarters, Sotheby's Auction House, and Bear Stearns's World Headquarters. Most recently he was made head foreman of the company for producing the highest rate of return per project.

Mr. Santarpia has always been involved in sports and fitness. He played linebacker for three years on his high school football team. As a young adult he was an amateur boxer and was a semifinalist in the 1991 New York Golden Gloves. He also trained young fighters in the Police Athletic League and the Bronx YMCA. He also coached peewee football for three years.

Having supervised and run major construction projects and having had his own carpentry company, Mr. Santarpia has gained the skills that will enable him to set up and operate the Powerhouse Gym. In addition he has the knowledge of running an operation with organization and efficiency. He will serve as the general manager and be responsible for the day-to-day operations.

Laura Augenti, Operations Manager

Ms. Augenti has been in the sales and management field for thirteen years. Starting out in the restaurant business at age eighteen, she worked her way up to dining room supervisor of Houlihan's restaurant in the Theatre District in New York City. After moving to Connecticut, she obtained a position as an assistant manager at a staffing agency at Vanguard Staffing. After one year she was promoted to sales manager, landing many large accounts such as Boehringer Ingelheim, IBM, and Honeywell Incorporated. Two years later Ms. Augenti was offered and accepted the position of branch manager, overseeing the entire Danbury office.

After moving back to New York, Ms. Augenti became an independent agent of a home-based travel agency (specializing in one destination).

Ms. Augenti has been involved in fitness and competition since high school, running track and playing volleyball. In college she played tennis and continued to run track. She ran the Walt Disney World Marathon in 2002, finishing at 613 out of 4,055 women, and 119 out of 765 in her age division.

With a wealth of experience in sales, management, and customer service, Ms. Augenti will be an asset to the daily operations and success of Powerhouse Gym.

Your Business Plan

In the organization and staffing section of your business plan, you will write about your life experiences that relate to your personal training business—the "path," if you will, that lead you to this point of forging ahead to start your own business.

Use the above content as a guide. Are you currently a personal trainer? Have you worked or do you still work in a fitness facility? What sports, if any, have you been involved in? Have you competed in any sports-related events or races? Do you have any management experience? Even if your business is just you, you will still be "managing" yourself and your business.

Profit and Loss

Under this section I have four subsections:

1. Projected Membership
2. Projected Income
3. Cash Flow
4. Summary of Financial Need

Projected Membership

Your projected membership will be your projected number of clients. Make a chart or graph of how many clients you will have at the beginning, at one year, at two years, and so on. It can look as simple as this:

Projected Cumulative Number of Clients
Year 1: 25
Year 2: 35
Year 3: 40

Projected Income

Create a chart to show this information. Again, it can be as simple as this (see, this doesn't have to be too scary):

	Year 1	Year 2	Year 3
Revenue	$88,000	$97,000	$106,000
Expenses	$37,000	$43,000	$49,000
EBITA*	$51,000	$54,000	$57,000

*Earnings Before Interest, Taxes, Depreciation, Amortization

Cash Flow

Your cash flow is basically where your money (income) came from (inflow or cash receipts) and where it went (outflow, or cash paid). In other words, your cash flow statement is your financial statement.

Here is a simple example of a cash flow statement. You can break down the different categories, to be as detailed as you want.

Statement of Cash Flow *(very simple example)*
One-year period (January 2010—December 2010)

Cash Flow from Operations: $65,000
Cash Flow from Investing: $(3,000)
Cash Flow from Financing: $(5,000)

Net Increase (Decrease) in Cash: $57,000

Summary of Financial Need

This section is just what it sounds like: a summary of your financial need. Here is an example: The start-up requirements (see chapter 6) are $42,500. This will cover the build-out of the existing shell location, equipment, computer/software, inventory, licenses, professional fees, and working capital.

05

Getting Started

What Type of Corporation Should You Formulate?

Although I have had two corporations, I am by no means an expert on forming them or deciding what type to form. Since I always go to my expert CPA for this type of advice, I decided who better than my CPA to advise you!

Mitchel Seidman, CPA, of Danbury, Connecticut, says: "I would advise a client to set up a corporation or limited liability company (LLC). Although sole proprietorships are the simplest form of business type, they leave owners with unlimited liability.

"Corporations are more complex than sole proprietorships in that a new legal entity is created. A corporation is an entity that is separate from its owners, so that regardless of what happens to shareholders, the corporation continues until it is dissolved. The owners of a corporation are known as shareholders. Taxation of corporations is much more complex than sole proprietorships. Depending on the number of, residency of, and type of shareholders, a corporation can elect to be treated for tax purposes as if it were a limited liability partnership (an S corporation) and therefore not pay taxes itself, or it can be treated as a taxable entity (a C corporation).

"LLC members have limited liability and can elect to be taxed either as corporations or as partners (if they have two or more members) or be disregarded for tax purposes like a sole proprietorship. Depending on state law, an LLC can have the same limited liability for members as a corporation, have some members with limited liability and some without limited liability (like a limited partnership), or even have no limited liability for any members (like a general partnership).

"The individual starting the business should consult a CPA or tax lawyer who can advise if an LLC, S corporation, or C corporation is ideal for them. What's more, state tax laws help determine the appropriate entity to use."

Here are two different forms that are used for paying "estimated" taxes throughout the year. The purpose is to not owe a high amount at the end of the year. Your CPA will advise you on which form to use.

2009 Estimated Tax Worksheet
Keep for Your Records

1	Adjusted gross income you expect in 2009 (see instructions below)	**1**
2	• If you plan to itemize deductions, enter the estimated total of your itemized deductions. **Caution:** *If line 1 above is over $166,800 ($83,400 if married filing separately), your deduction may be reduced. See Pub. 505 for details.* • If you do not plan to itemize deductions, enter your standard deduction from page 1 or Pub. 505, Worksheet 2-3.	**2**
3	Subtract line 2 from line 1	**3**
4	Exemptions. Multiply $3,650 by the number of personal exemptions. **Caution:** *See Pub. 505 to figure the amount to enter if line 1 above is over: $250,200 if married filing jointly or qualifying widow(er); $208,500 if head of household; $166,800 if single; or $125,100 if married filing separately*	**4**
5	Subtract line 4 from line 3	**5**
6	**Tax.** Figure your tax on the amount on line 5 by using the **2009 Tax Rate Schedules** on page 5. **Caution:** *If you will have qualified dividends or a net capital gain, or expect to claim the foreign earned income exclusion or housing exclusion, see Pub. 505 to figure the tax*	**6**
7	Alternative minimum tax from **Form 6251**	**7**
8	Add lines 6 and 7. Add to this amount any other taxes you expect to include in the total on Form 1040, line 44, or Form 1040A, line 28	**8**
9	Credits (see instructions below). **Do not** include any income tax withholding on this line	**9**
10	Subtract line 9 from line 8. If zero or less, enter -0-	**10**
11	Self-employment tax (see instructions below). Estimate of 2009 net earnings from self-employment $_____ ; if **$106,800 or less**, multiply the amount by 15.3%; if **more than $106,800**, multiply the amount by 2.9%, add $13,243.20 to the result, and enter the total. **Caution:** *If you also have wages subject to social security tax or the 6.2% portion of tier 1 Railroad Retirement tax, see Pub. 505 to figure the amount to enter*	**11**
12	Other taxes (see instructions below)	**12**
13a	Add lines 10 through 12	**13a**
b	Earned income credit, additional child tax credit, and credits from **Forms 4136, 5405, 8801 (line 27),** and **8885**	**13b**
c	**Total 2009 estimated tax.** Subtract line 13b from line 13a. If zero or less, enter -0- . . . . . ▶	**13c**
14a	Multiply line 13c by 90% (66⅔ % for farmers and fishermen) . . . . . [14a]	
b	Enter the tax shown on your 2008 tax return (110% of that amount if you are not a farmer or fisherman and the adjusted gross income shown on that return is more than $150,000 or, if married filing separately for 2009, more than $75,000) [14b]	
c	**Required annual payment to avoid a penalty.** Enter the **smaller** of line 14a or 14b . . . . . ▶	**14c**
	Caution: *Generally, if you do not prepay (through income tax withholding and estimated tax payments) at least the amount on line 14c, you may owe a penalty for not paying enough estimated tax. To avoid a penalty, make sure your estimate on line 13c is as accurate as possible. Even if you pay the required annual payment, you may still owe tax when you file your return. If you prefer, you can pay the amount shown on line 13c. For details, see Pub. 505.*	
15	Income tax withheld and estimated to be withheld during 2009 (including income tax withholding on pensions, annuities, certain deferred income, etc.)	**15**
16a	Subtract line 15 from line 14c . . . . . . [16a]	
	Is the result zero or less?	
	☐ **Yes.** Stop here. You are not required to make estimated tax payments.	
	☐ **No.** Go to line 16b.	
b	Subtract line 15 from line 13c . . . . . . [16b]	
	Is the result less than $1,000?	
	☐ **Yes.** Stop here. You are not required to make estimated tax payments.	
	☐ **No.** Go to line 17 to figure your required payment.	
17	If the first payment you are required to make is due April 15, 2009, enter ¼ of line 16a (minus any 2008 overpayment that you are applying to this installment) here, and on your estimated tax payment voucher(s) if you are paying by check or money order. (**Note:** *Household employers, see instructions below.*)	**17**

Instructions for the 2009 Estimated Tax Worksheet

Line 1. Adjusted gross income. Use your 2008 tax return and instructions as a guide to figuring the adjusted gross income you expect in 2009 (but be sure to consider the items listed under *What's New* that begins on page 1). For more details on figuring your adjusted gross income, see *Expected AGI—Line 1* in chapter 2 of Pub. 505. If you are self-employed, be sure to take into account the deduction for one-half of your self-employment tax (2008 Form 1040, line 27).

Line 9. Credits. See the 2008 Form 1040, lines 47 through 54, or Form 1040A, lines 29 through 33, and the related instructions.

Line 11. Self-employment tax. If you and your spouse make joint estimated tax payments and you both have self-employment income, figure the self-employment tax for each of you separately. Enter the total on line 11. When figuring your estimate of 2009 net earnings from self-employment, be sure to use only 92.35% (.9235) of your total net profit from self-employment.

Line 12. Other taxes. Use the instructions for the 2008 Form 1040 to determine if you expect to owe, for 2009, any of the taxes that would have been entered on your 2008 Form 1040, lines 59 (additional tax on early distributions only) and 60, and any write-ins on line 61, or any amount from Form 1040A, line 36. On line 12, enter the total of those taxes, subject to the following two exceptions.

Exception 1. Include household employment taxes from box b of Form 1040, line 60, on this line only if:

• You will have federal income tax withheld from wages, pensions, annuities, gambling winnings, or other income, or

• You would be required to make estimated tax payments (to avoid a penalty) even if you did not include household employment taxes when figuring your estimated tax.

If you meet one or both of the above, include in the amount on line 12 the total of your household employment taxes before subtracting advance EIC payments made to your employee(s).

Exception 2. Of the amounts for other taxes that may be entered on Form 1040, line 61, do not include on line 12: tax on recapture of a federal mortgage subsidy, uncollected employee social security and Medicare tax or RRTA tax on tips or group-term life insurance, tax on golden parachute payments, look-back interest due under section 167(g) or 460(b), or excise tax on insider stock compensation from an expatriated corporation. These taxes are not required to be paid until the due date of your income tax return (not including extensions).

Repayment of first-time homebuyer credit. If you claimed the first-time homebuyer credit for 2008 and the home ceased to be your main home in 2009, you generally must include on line 12 the entire credit you claimed for 2008. This includes situations where you sell the home or convert it to business or rental property. See Form 5405 for exceptions.

Line 17. If you are a household employer and you make advance EIC payments to your employee(s), reduce your required estimated tax payment for each period by the amount of advance EIC payments paid during the period.

-4-

Form **1120-W**

(WORKSHEET)

Department of the Treasury
Internal Revenue Service

• • • •• • • • • • • • ••• ••• • •• • •• ••• • •

For calendar year 2009, or tax year beginning .... , 2009, and ending .... , 20 .....

(Keep for the corporation's records—Do *not* send to the Internal Revenue Service.)

OMB No. 1545-0975

2009

Part I   **Estimated Tax Computation**

1	Taxable income expected for the tax year	**1**
	Qualified personal service corporations (defined in the instructions), skip lines 2 through 13 and go to line 14. Members of a controlled group, see instructions.	
2	Enter the **smaller** of line 1 or $50,000	**2**
3	Multiply line 2 by 15%	**3**
4	Subtract line 2 from line 1	**4**
5	Enter the **smaller** of line 4 or $25,000	**5**
6	Multiply line 5 by 25%	**6**
7	Subtract line 5 from line 4	**7**
8	Enter the **smaller** of line 7 or $9,925,000	**8**
9	Multiply line 8 by 34%	**9**
10	Subtract line 8 from line 7	**10**
11	Multiply line 10 by 35%	**11**
12	If line 1 is greater than $100,000, enter the **smaller** of **(a)** 5% of the excess over $100,000 or **(b)** $11,750. Otherwise, enter -0-	**12**
13	If line 1 is greater than $15 million, enter the **smaller** of **(a)** 3% of the excess over $15 million or **(b)** $100,000. Otherwise, enter -0-	**13**
14	Add lines 3, 6, 9, and 11 through 13. (Qualified personal service corporations, multiply line 1 by 35%.)	**14**
15	Alternative tax. If the corporation has qualified timber gain, complete Part II and enter the amount from line 37 here. Otherwise, skip lines 15 and 16 and go to line 17	**15**
16	Enter smaller of line 14 or line 15	**16**
17	Alternative minimum tax (see instructions)	**17**
18	**Total.** If the corporation has qualified timber gain, add lines 16 and 17. Otherwise, add lines 14 and 17	**18**
19	Tax credits (see instructions)	**19**
20	Subtract line 19 from line 18	**20**
21	Other taxes (see instructions)	**21**
22	**Total tax.** Add lines 20 and 21	**22**
23	Credit for federal tax paid on fuels (see instructions)	**23**
24	Subtract line 23 from line 22. **Note:** *If the result is less than $500, the corporation is not required to make estimated tax payments*	**24**
25a	Enter the tax shown on the corporation's 2008 tax return (see instructions). **Caution:** *If the tax is zero or the tax year was for less than 12 months, skip this line and enter the amount from line 24 on line 25b*	**25a**
b	Enter the **smaller** of line 24 or line 25a. If the corporation is required to skip line 25a, enter the amount from line 24	**25b**

		(a)	(b)	(c)	(d)
26	**Installment due dates** (see instructions) . . . . . ▶ **26**				
27	**Required installments.** Enter 25% of line 25b in columns **(a)** through **(d)** unless the corporation uses the annualized income installment method or adjusted seasonal installment method or is a "large corporation" (see instructions) **27**				

For Paperwork Reduction Act Notice, see instructions.   Cat. No. 11525G   Form **1120-W** (2009)

How to Obtain a Federal Tax Identification Number

For tax purposes and reporting, you will need a Federal Tax Identification Number, also known as an Employer Identification Number (EIN). Applying for an EIN is simple. You can do it online in five minutes by filling out a form. Just visit www.gov-tax.com or www.irs.gov/businesses/small/article/0,,id=102767,00.html. The site will first ask you what type of corporation you have, and then you can fill out the appropriate form.

The form will ask questions such as your name, business name, type of entity (corporation), and principal activity of the business (you can check "other" and write in "personal training").

Immediately after completing the application, you will receive your EIN. You can then use this to open your business bank account, apply for a business license, and file your tax returns.

Obtaining a Business License

Most city, county, and state governments require all business owners to obtain a business license. This is a general license that allows you to operate your business legally, within your jurisdiction.

To obtain a business license, first contact your city hall or county government office to find out what type of license you need (ask if you need a local and/or a state license). They will be able to give you the necessary application to get started. To fill out the application, you will need to have your paperwork, including your EIN number and trade name (if applicable) certificate.

Once you have completed the application, file it with your city hall or government office. You will also pay a fee at this time. Each year, you will need to renew your license and pay the fee. It's a good idea to get this on your calendar so you don't forget.

Branding Your Business

Branding your business means getting your business known and recognized in the world (or at least in your community). Don't let the word scare you; this is not an additional time-consuming element. It is something that is and always has been a very important part of building a business. Branding groups together key elements of business ownership. It means building your company to the standards that you have set for yourself and keeping those standards up. Once you have

Links for Where to Obtain a State Business License

Alabama: www.ador.state.al.us/licenses/authrity.html

Alaska: www.dced.state.ak.us/occ/buslic.htm

Arizona: www.revenue.state.az.us/609/licensingguide.htm

Arkansas: www.arkansas.gov/business_res.php

California: www.calgold.ca.gov

Colorado: www.colorado.gov/cs/Satellite/CO-Portal/CXP/1165693060265

Connecticut: www.state.ct.us

Delaware: www.state.de.us/revenue/services/Business_Tax/Step3.shtml

District of Columbia: www.dcra.dc.gov

Florida: http://sun6.dms.state.fl.us/dor/businesses

Georgia: www.sos.state.ga.us/corporations/regforms.htm

Hawaii: www.hawaii.gov/dbedt/business/start_grow

Idaho: www.idoc.state.id.us/Pages/BUSINESSPAGE.html

Illinois: www.business.illinois.gov/licenses.cfm

Indiana: www.in.gov/sos/business/2428.htm

Iowa: http://iowalifechanging.com/business/blic.html /

Kansas: www.accesskansas.org/businesscenter/index.html?link=maintain#license renewals

Kentucky: www.thinkkentucky.com/BIC/ebpermits.aspx

Louisiana: http://louisiana.gov/Business

Maine: www.maine.gov/portal/business/licensing.html

Maryland: www.dllr.state.md.us

Massachusetts: www.state.ma.us/sec/cor/coridx.htm

Michigan: www.michigan.gov/som/0,1607,7-192-29943_31469_31893---,00 .html

Minnesota: www.state.mn.us/portal/mn/jsp/home.do?agency=LicenseMN

Mississippi: www.olemiss.edu/depts/mssbdc/going_intobus.html

Missouri: www.missouribusiness.net/docs/license_registration_checklist.asp

Montana: http://sos.mt.gov

Nebraska: http://assist.neded.org/licensed.html

Nevada: http://nv.gov/DoingBusiness_nevada.htm

New Hampshire: www.nh.gov/business/doingbusiness.html

New Jersey: www.state.nj.us/njbusiness/licenses

New Mexico: Not available at this time

New York: www.dos.state.ny.us/lcns/licensing.html

North Carolina: www.nccommerce.com/en/BusinessServices/StartYourBusiness/BusinessLicensesPermits

North Dakota: www.nd.gov/sos/businessserv/registrations/business-search.html

Ohio: www.sos.state.oh.us/SOS/businessServices.aspx

Oklahoma: www.okonestop.com

Oregon: www.filinginoregon.com

Pennsylvania: www.paopenforbusiness.state.pa.us

Rhode Island: www.dlt.ri.gov/lmi/jobseeker/license.htm

South Carolina: http://sc.gov/Portal/Category/BUSINESS_TOP

South Dakota: www.state.sd.us/drr2/newbusiness.htm

Tennessee: www.tennesseeanytime.org/business/index.html

Texas: www.texasonline.com/portal/tol/en/gov/9

Utah: www.utah.gov/business

Vermont: www.vermont.gov/portal/business

Virginia: www.virginia.gov/cmsportal3/business_4096/index.html

Washington: www.dol.wa.gov/business/licensing.html

West Virginia: www.wvtax.gov/businessRegistrationTaxForms.html

Wisconsin: www.wdfi.org/corporations/forms/

Wyoming: http://soswy.state.wy.us/Business/Business.aspx

established your brand, it is of utmost importance to work at keeping it where you want it.

Following are several key components to building and maintaining your brand.

Customer Service

Customer service is an extremely important component of building your brand (and keeping it!). As your own boss, there is no one to discipline you but yourself, so you might find it easy to break the rules. Your business will suffer if you do this! If you are in a bad mood, can't shake it, and your phone rings, don't answer it. Let your client leave a message and call him or her back when you are able to have a happy, patient, and kind voice. Think about if you had an employee (which you may in the future); how would you want him or her to provide customer service? You should expect the same (or more) from yourself at all times.

Advertising

You know you will have to advertise your business in some way or another. But you may be thinking that you will advertise for a short while and then you won't have

Real-Life Story

Branding can be acquired in so many ways. Using your creativity can open up a world of options. Before we even opened our Powerhouse Gym on Maui in 2005—when Jerry and I were still in the planning stages, no lease yet, still looking for a location—we decided to start the mission of branding. We wanted to make an impression on the community and put ourselves in the front of their minds.

Before we went to Maui to look for a location for our gym, meet with realtors, and so on, we had one hundred T-shirts made. We put the Powerhouse Gym logo on them, along with the word *Maui* right below it. When we got to Maui, we handed out the T-shirts to locals whom we met during our ten-day trip, including bartenders, servers, and anyone else we met who lived in the town in which we were opening the gym. We spoke to as many people as we could and created a buzz. So before we even opened our doors, one hundred people were walking around town in our T-shirts, making it known that we were coming and opening our business.

to anymore . . . wrong! Advertising consistently is a must. Your clients and potential clients will notice if they see you have a newspaper ad, maybe some fliers around town, even radio ads, and then all of the sudden it stops. This will lessen your credibility, and it will allow your business to fade from people's minds. You will want to stay fresh in people's minds all the time, and you do that by advertising.

Public Relations

You may have heard the phrase "public relations" without ever really knowing what it means. Public relations are the actions of an individual or business to promote goodwill between itself and the public, the community, employees, customers, and so on.

One way to establish good public relations is to get involved in your community through volunteer work; helping others is an excellent way to establish yourself in the community as a trustworthy and all-around good person. Giving back to your community may also help you get some free press. If you make a commitment to volunteer or otherwise help your community, however, you have to treat that commitment very seriously and always do what you say you are going to do. For example, if you volunteer to help at a school event, with a local charity, or at a local children's sporting event, be sure to keep that commitment.

Creating a Logo

Small businesses often fail as a result of sloppy or half-baked advertising. Creating a logo and using it on all of your printed materials and advertising will provide your business with professionalism and credibility. Many small businesses do not create a logo, thinking it is unnecessary and an easy way to cut corners. But having a logo

Where to Get a Custom Logo

Getting a custom logo is actually pretty simple. You can simply go online to www.logomaker.com and get one for just $49. Once you get to the site, pick out a custom logo—they currently have over ten thousand to choose from. You then customize the logo with colors, your business name, and the fonts of your choice. Next, save your logo and try it out online. Once you are happy with your custom logo, you can buy it. It couldn't be easier—and it's fun!

shows your customers and potential customers that you are serious—that your business is professional and here to stay.

Forms and Charts

There are several forms and charts you will need to help you keep track of your clients. Some you will fill out before you start training each client, and some you will use over the course of time you train each client.

Forms to Use Prior to Training Clients

- **Assessment.** The purpose of this form is to help you get to know your clients before you start training them. You can use it to find out if they have any injuries or limitations, as well as what their goals are.
- **Training Agreement.** This form has the clients' contact information, how many sessions they purchased, expiration dates, and cancellation policy. You can also include the liability waiver on this form.
- **Waiver and Release.** This is a liability form that your clients sign prior to training with you. It waives your responsibility if they should get injured and protects you against potential lawsuits.
- **Medical Release.** This form is for any clients who may be at risk for a medical condition that may be aggravated by exercise. If your clients mention a medical condition, or if they are a male over the age of forty-five or a female over the age of fifty, I recommend having their doctor sign a medical release form. These ages are just a recommendation; you can go younger or older if you choose.

Forms to Use Throughout Training

- **Training Log.** Use this form to track each session. Be sure to add the date and time each time you use it.
- **Workout Chart.** This chart is used to keep track of your clients' workouts. It is impossible to remember what each client did the last time he or she had a session with you. Use the chart to track the workout routines as well as how much weight was used for each set.
- **Measurement Chart.** Use this chart to keep track of your clients' measurements. This will help you figure out where they need to work harder, or where they are making progress and are close to reaching their goals.

Keeping Records of Your Clients' Training

You can create and print all of the above forms yourself using Word or Excel. It is not necessary to have them printed professionally—except for the Training Agreement. The Training Agreement should have a second copy attached. When your clients fill out the form and sign the bottom, you then tear off the second copy and give it to your client. You keep the hard copy (top copy) for your records.

When you get a new client, create a file and then keep all of his or her forms and charts in this file. While, yes, we live in the computer age, there is still a need for paper in this business.

As you work with your client, update his or her charts and forms regularly. Each time you have a session, use the workout chart and training log. You may not use the progress chart each time. You might choose to use it every two or even every four weeks. If you use it every four weeks (or once a month), the results will likely be more dramatic, which in turn could keep your client motivated. On the other hand, some clients may need to keep up with their progress a little more closely if they have a tendency to slip backward in their progress. You will have to make this decision on an individual basis.

You can keep some information on the computer, such as a database to keep your clients' contact info.

Maintenance and Repair of Equipment

Maintaining your equipment should be a high priority. Inspect your equipment on a weekly basis. Make sure all dumbbells or barbells are tight (no loose weights on the ends). Check the cables on your strength equipment, ensuring they are tight, lubricated, and in satisfactory working order.

On your cardio equipment, look and listen for loose fasteners or unusual sounds every day. If you notice anything wrong or different, obtain service as soon as possible. Make sure fit balls have adequate air.

Clean the equipment thoroughly with disinfectant after each use—especially cardio equipment and benches.

Every two to three months, open up the cardio equipment and vacuum the motors and circuit boards.

Date _____ Time_____ am/pm Source _____ Fitness Counselor _____

GENERAL ORIENTATION

Name _____ Age _____ Birth date _____/_____/_____ Male _____ Female _____

Address _____ City _____ St. _____ Zip_____

Day Phone _____ Evening Phone _____ E-mail _____

Employer _____ Emergency Contact _____ Phone _____

Doctor's Name _____ Phone _____

PHYSICAL ACTIVITY READINESS

YES NO
☐ ☐ 1. Has your doctor ever said you have heart trouble?
☐ ☐ 2. Do you frequently have pains in your heart or chest?
☐ ☐ 3. Do you often feel faint or have spells of severe dizziness?
☐ ☐ 4. Has a doctor ever said your blood pressure was too high?
☐ ☐ 5. Has your doctor ever told you that you have a bone or joint problem
        such as arthritis that has been aggravated by exercise or
        might be worse with exercise?
☐ ☐ 6. Is there a good physical reason not mentioned here why you
        should not follow an activity program even if you wanted to?
☐ ☐ 7. Are you over age 65 and not accustomed to vigorous exercise?
☐ ☐ 8. Have you consulted your physician regarding increasing your physical activity and/or taking a fitness evaluation?
☐ ☐ 9. If No to question 8, will you consult your physician prior to increasing your physical activity and/or taking a fitness evaluation?

YES NO
☐ ☐ Smoker?
☐ ☐ Diabetes?
☐ ☐ Family history of heart disease?
☐ ☐ Back/Knee/Sacroiliac Problems?
☐ ☐ High Blood Pressure?
☐ ☐ Recent Surgery?
☐ ☐ Asthma (uncontrolled)?

*If yes to any of the above, please see Fitness
Counselor before exercise is scheduled.*

MEMBER EVALUATION

Fitness Goal _____ Secondary Fitness Goal _____

Present weight _____ lbs. Years at present weight _____ Highest weight _____ Desired weight _____ lbs.

Have you ever participated in a weight loss/gain program? _____ When were you in the best shape of your life? _____

What activities are you presently involved in? _____

How many times a day do you eat, including snacks? _____ When do you eat your first meal?_____ Last meal?_____

Do you feel drops in your energy level during the day? _____ Time? _____

Approximately how many calories do you eat per day (average)? _____ Do you take vitamins or supplements (type)? _____

How much cardio exercise (min.) do you do a day (average)? _____ Weight training? _____ Sports? _____

Have you ever worked with a fitness professional or personal trainer? _____ How would it be beneficial for you? _____

Realistically, how many times per week does exercise fit into your lifestyle? _____

FITNESS GOALS

What makes this time better than other times in your life to start reaching for your goals? _____

What stopped you last time? _____

What would you specifically like to change physically? _____

Why is that important to you? _____

Motivation level to achieve present goal? 1 2 3 4 5 6 7 8 9 10

What is your time frame to achieve your goal? _____ Do you have an exact plan to achieve your goal? _____

I certify the above statements are true and correct to the best of my knowledge. _____

Signature

Doctor's note requested _____/_____/_____ IF REQUESTED Received _____/_____/_____ DO NOT PROCEED UNLESS NOTE IS RECEIVED

Circuit 5-minute warm-up + 20-minute strength circuit + 20 minutes of cardio = 45 minutes (Get in, Get fit, Get out!)

Name:

Strength Training Exercise*	Date>										
Leg Press	lbs.										
	reps.										
Leg Curl	lbs.										
	reps.										
Leg Extension	lbs.										
	reps.										
Chest Press	lbs.										
	reps.										
Seated Row	lbs.										
	reps.										
Shoulder Press	lbs.										
	reps.										
Lat Pulldown	lbs.										
	reps.										
Lateral Raise	lbs.										
	reps.										
Triceps Extension	lbs.										
	reps.										
Biceps Curl	lbs.										
	reps.										
Abdominal	lbs.										
	reps.										
Back Extension	lbs.										
	reps.										

Notes:

*Warm up for 5 minutes on a piece of cardiovascular equipment prior to starting the Life Fitness Powerhouse Circuit. The Life Fitness Cross-Trainer provides an excellent total-body warm-up.

Perform the **strength training** exercises every other day (at least 2 to 3 times per week). Once you have the hang of it, this 12-piece circuit should take about 20 minutes to complete (even faster when no one else is around). It should take you around 90 seconds to set up and complete one set at each station.

POWERHOUSE Cardio and Others

Cardiovascular Exercise	Date>							
Treadmill	Time							
	Distance							
	Calories							
Cross-Trainer	Time							
	Distance							
	Calories							
LifeCycle	Time							
	Distance							
	Calories							
Stair Climber	Time							
	Distance							
	Calories							
Other								
	Time							
	Distance							
	Calories							
Body Weight								
	Reps							
	Reps							
	Reps							
Stretching								
Chest								
Shoulder								
Upper Back								
Lower Back								
Hamstrings								
Quadriceps								
Biceps								
Triceps								
Calves								

Notes:

Cardiovascular workouts can be conducted every day with the Powerhouse Circuit. Variety is extremely important for both your body and your mind. Try new pieces from time to time—you may find a new favorite. Work yourself up to 20 minutes of cardiovascular activity.

Stretch only after you have warmed up; never stretch a cold muscle. Stretching at the end of the workout can help you to slow down and cool down. It will also give you some time to think about what you have to do after you leave the Powerhouse Gym.

Laura's Studio

123 Main St.
Anytown, USA 12345
914-555-1212

PERSONAL INFORMATION

Last Name	First Name	Member #
Address		Barcode #
City, State, Zip		Driver's License #
Home Phone	Work Phone	DOB
		☐ Male ☐ Female
E-mail Address		
Employer		Source
Emergency Contact Name	Relation	Emergency Contact Phone

PERSONAL TRAINING

Sessions Purchased:

Cost of Sessions: $ _____
Surcharges/Fees/Other: $ _____
Total Due Today: $ _____

Sessions Begin:
Sessions Expire:
Deposit: $ _____
Balance: $ _____

Payment Method: ☐ Cash   ☐ Check   ☐ Credit Card

TERMS AND CONDITIONS

I agree to the following terms and conditions relating to this Personal Training agreement ("Agreement"):

1. I understand that any and all recommended exercises are voluntary and I can refuse to participate in any or all of the recommended exercises.
2. All training sessions are non-transferable and non-refundable. I understand that I must give the training staff and/or my scheduled personal trainer at least 24 hours' notice to cancel a training session. If I do not give at least 24 hours' notice, I may or may not, at the discretion of my personal trainer, forfeit that session(s).
3. All sessions must be completed on or before the Agreement expiration date, unless valid military or medical proof is provided.
4. Member must sign for each session at the time of his/her workout, including session(s) cancelled without 24 hours' notice. Laura's Studio reserves the right to provide a substitute personal trainer in the event that the scheduled trainer is unavailable to conduct a session.
5. All standard terms and conditions of my membership agreement are incorporated in and made a part of this agreement.

LEGAL GUARDIAN

Any member who is under the age of 18 must have a parent or legal guardian ("Legal Guardian") co-sign this agreement. The Legal Guardian shall be jointly and severely liable for any and all obligations of such member hereunder and shall be bound by all the terms and conditions of this agreement.

Name of Legal Guardian: _____   Signature: _____

Address: _____

RELEASE OF LIABILITY • BUYER'S RIGHT TO CANCEL

Using Laura's Studio involves the risk of injury to you or your guest, whether you or someone else causes it. Specific risks vary from one activity to another and the risks range from minor injuries to major injuries, such as catastrophic injuries including death. **In consideration of your participation in the activities offered by Laura's Studio, you understand and voluntarily accept this risk and agree that Laura's Studio, its officers, directors, employees, volunteers, agents, and independent contractors, will not be liable for any injury, including, without limitation, personal, bodily, or mental injury, economic loss or any damage to you, your spouse, guests, unborn child, or relatives resulting from the negligence of Laura's Studio or anyone on Laura's Studio's behalf or anyone using the Facilities, whether related to exercise or not.** Further, you understand and acknowledge that Laura's Studio does not manufacture fitness or other equipment at its Facilities, but purchases and/or leases equipment. You understand and acknowledge that Laura's Studio is providing recreational services and may not be held liable for defective products. By signing below, you acknowledge and agree that you have read the foregoing and know of the nature of the activities at Laura's Studio and you agree to all the terms on the front and back pages of this agreement and acknowledge you have received a copy of it and the membership policies.

NOTICE TO PURCHASER: DO NOT SIGN THIS CONTRACT UNTIL YOU READ BOTH SIDES OR IF IT CONTAINS BLANK SPACES. IF YOU DECIDE YOU DO NOT WISH TO REMAIN A CLIENT OF LAURA'S STUDIO, YOU MAY CANCEL THIS CONTRACT BY MAILING TO LAURA'S STUDIO BY MIDNIGHT OF THE THIRD BUSINESS DAY AFTER YOU SIGN THIS CONTRACT A NOTICE STATING YOUR DESIRE TO CANCEL THIS CONTRACT. THE WRITTEN NOTICE MUST BE MAILED BY CERTIFIED MAIL TO THE FOLLOWING ADDRESS: 123 MAIN ST., ANYTOWN, USA 12345

Client Signature: _____   Date: _____   Employee Name: _____   ID #: _____

Equipment Maintenance Checklist

	Mon	Tues	Wed	Thurs	Fri	Sat	Sun
Wipe Down Cardio							
Check Dumbbells for Tightness							
Check Multifunctional Trainer							
Check Cardio for Noise/Loose Parts							
Check Bench Wipe Down							
Check Fit Balls for Air Clean							
Clean Floor Mats							

06 Financial Planning

Here comes the part that is not usually the most fun in opening and running your business. Although if you have enough money to run your business smoothly, it actually can be fun! Financial planning is key and cannot be ignored.

I will cover your financial planning in every aspect, from spending to collecting. In order to run a successful business, you have to learn to plan for your spending and keep track of your spending.

Cost of Equipment

I discussed equipment in chapter 3 and included the approximate costs of most of the equipment you will need to purchase. Here I will give a brief overview focusing only on cost.

The cost of two pieces of cardio equipment ranges from $6,000 to $24,000. I realize that this is a big range; you should expect to spend somewhere in the middle. When I discuss financial management in chapter 7, you will have a better understanding of what your budget will be for equipment costs, whether or not you will want to take out a loan, and so on. Once you know your budget for equipment spending, you can decide whether to purchase refurbished equipment or new and how much equipment you can buy to start up your business.

Purchasing Your Equipment

For your large (or major) equipment purchases—strength and cardio—the vendors have sales reps for their commercial lines. So, if you decide to go with the higher-end commercial equipment, you should be ready to negotiate.

Example: Say "vendor A" gives you a price for a treadmill of $7,500, and "vendor B" gives you a price on their brand of the same grade treadmill of

---

Keeping Track of Equipment Costs

- Treadmill: Refurbished: $1,500; New: $8,000

- Elliptical: Refurbished: $1,200; New: $5,500

- Functional Trainer: Refurbished: $2,000; New $6,000

- Bench: $450–$750

- Dumbbells with Rack: $600–$2,000

- Stability Balls: three balls: $70

- Stability Ball Wall Rack: $70

- Two Floor Mats: $50

- Additional Exercise Accessories: $300–$1,000

$7,000. Go back to "vendor A" and and let him know that you can get a similar treadmill for $500 less than his price. Nine times out of ten, "vendor A" will meet the price, and maybe go down even more.

If you buy your major equipment (your cardio and strength) from one vendor, this will give you more bargaining power. You may even get some "freebies" thrown in. Don't be afraid to negotiate.

It is also a great idea to get to know the sales reps. A good way to do this is by going to the trade shows to meet them personally.

Start-Up Costs

I will cover everything you will need to get your business started. It is necessary to plan this out so that you know how much money you will need and so you can be sure you do not overspend. There are many items you probably would not include in your budget if you left it all just floating around in your head.

We are all in business to make money—that is for certain. This means you will need to bring in more money than you spend. Simple, right? Not always. A high percentage of small businesses fail because of poor (or lack of) financial planning,

Start-Up Costs	
Cardiovascular and Strength-Training Equipment	$25,000
Accessories (Equipment)	$750
Build-out Construction	$10,000
Insurance	$2,000
Initial Marketing and Web Design	$3,000
Computer Equipment and Software	$1,500
Total	**$42,250**

meaning they do not take the time to create a budget, project spending, and then stick to their budget. Sometimes it is inevitable that you will spend more than you plan to. For instance, your elliptical might need servicing that you cannot do yourself, so you will have to pay someone to fix it. However, in every budget you should also plan for unexpected costs.

Creating lists and spreadsheets is the best way to project and keep track of your finances.

First Things First

I spoke about getting started, acquiring your business license, formulating your corporation, getting your logo, and so on. All of these things will cost money. As you may already know (if not, you will soon learn), there are not a lot of free things out there. Make sure to include these costs in your start-up costs.

Office Supplies

I covered furniture and office supplies and what you will need to get started. Figuring out the cost of these items is the next step. The costs will not be exact, but try to estimate as close as possible. If anything, estimate on the high side. It is better to be under budget than to underestimate and then go over budget.

There are ways to cut down costs in this department. If you already have a desk, use it. If you already have a computer, use that one for now. To keep costs down in the beginning, make a list of everything you will need. Then look around . . . how much of this stuff do you already have? If you can use supplies and furniture that you already have, then do that. Once you are up and running, if you are bringing in the dollars and it fits in your budget, you can go out and replace your old stuff with new if you want to.

How Much to Charge Your Clients

A mistake that personal trainers (or anyone in a service-oriented business) often make is thinking they have to charge what everyone else is charging. That is not the case. What are you offering? Won't you be striving to be the best? Of course you will be, and that's why you must check out what the majority of trainers are charging, make sure you offer a better service, and make sure you are worth every penny!

How is it that some doctors charge more for a breast augmentation than others? Well, the doctors with the highest credentials and most respected reputation can charge more.

The key is to make yourself such a commodity that people will beg to pay you. Okay, so maybe they won't beg, but they should want to pay you and feel that it is a privilege to have you as their trainer.

Set yourself apart from your competition. Don't be a trainer who just counts reps; those trainers are a dime a dozen. Be a trainer who is hands-on, be creative, get your clients excited, make them want to come back for more.

Once you have figured out your expenses, your monthly budget, and how much you will need to make a living, then you can calculate how much you should be charging per session.

Your Place on the Map Plays a Part

If you live in a large city such as New York or Los Angeles versus a small town, you will be able to justify different price structures. So, yes, what your competition is charging does play a part in your decision to a degree. If the average personal trainer is charging $50 per session, and the range is $40 to $60, you will not want to charge $70; that is just unrealistic.

Your price point should be realistic in relation to what you are offering. If you know you are a dedicated, knowledgeable trainer who motivates, resulting in your clients getting results and enjoying their time with you, then you should charge on the high end of the average. If (and I shudder to say this) you are a trainer who is average in a pool of trainers—maybe your clients are not getting a lot of motivation—then you should start out charging in the middle range. However, I can say "start out" because I expect that you would work to get to the top of the ladder as one of *the* best, or the best, trainer in your area.

Create Packages, Sell More

Offering a variety of choices for your clients may be an option you wish to explore. You can opt to have one set price per session—across the board. Or you can create packages for different client needs.

You can give your clients the option to pay you per session, or you can sell them packages of five sessions for a small discount. If they purchase a package of ten sessions, perhaps the discount could be even deeper. If you sell a package at a discount rate, you have the client pay for the entire package up front. You may get slightly less money overall, but in the long run this could work to your advantage, as you know you have a steady client.

Creating a Payment Policy and Sticking to It

All businesses have a payment policy, or *should* have one. If you do not have a clear payment policy, you are opening the door for your clients to walk all over you. There are plenty of stories out there of clients who say, "I'll pay you next time" or "I forgot my checkbook." If you allow this to go on, you will end up in big trouble. Your clients will not only not respect you, but they will also feel like they can take advantage of you—and they *will* take advantage of you.

An example of a payment policy would be that your clients must pay you before their session, or after their session, but absolutely at some point during the time

---

Advantages of Selling Prepaid Packages at a Discount

- Your client sees that you are flexible and offering options.

- You have now gotten a commitment from your client to come to you five or ten (or any number you wish to sell) times.

- Having your client commit to multiple sessions gives you time to motivate them and get them "addicted" to having you train them.

- You get the money up front, no guessing if your client will call to book another session or cancel a last-minute session that you now lost money on.

frame that they are with you. You can incorporate a policy where they pay for a certain number of sessions up front—that would be an example of selling packages.

You will not want to accept "I owe yous." Make your policy on this clear from the very beginning. The first time you meet with your client or potential client, explain in detail your policy. Don't be shy or scared to be firm about this. Being firm with your rules of payment will only validate that you are professional and serious about your business. This in turn will help in your clients' mental approach to committing to train with you for the long haul.

Creating a Budget

You may or may not have experience with creating a budget. If you have never had your own business, perhaps you have created a budget for your household

Monthly Budget

FIXED EXPENSES:

Rent or Mortgage   _____

Phone   _____

Utilities: Gas/Electric   _____

Insurance   _____

Internet Service   _____

Bookkeeper/Accounting   _____

VARIABLE EXPENSES:

Marketing and Advertising   _____

Printing Costs   _____

Postage   _____

Office Supplies   _____

Repairs and Maintenance   _____

Miscellaneous (can include cleaning supplies,
additional equipment, lightbulbs, etc.)   _____

finances. If you have never created a budget, don't worry. Like everything else, you can learn this too.

To begin creating your budget, formulate a list of all of your monthly expenses. This includes bills such as utilities, insurance, and advertising. On your yearly budget sheet, you will have columns for each month and for year-end totals. Here is an example of a monthly budget sheet:

Fixed Expenses

Fixed expenses are bills that do not change from month to month, or vary only very slightly. Examples of typical small business fixed expenses are loan payments, insurance, electricity, phone, and Internet access.

Fixed expenses do not fluctuate with the volume of business you do. There is very little or nothing you can do to change these bills. You may be extra cautious with your electricity usage, for example, but realistically you will not be able to change it to any great degree.

Variable Expenses

Variable expenses are your business expenses that will vary depending on your volume of business, sales, or transactions. Examples of variable expenses include food and entertainment and the cost of materials (equipment or cleaning supplies). Your variable expenses will fluctuate, and you will have control over them for the most part.

To Be Realistic or Not

Your start-up budget is truthfully just a guess. Before you are actually in business, you will be guessing, or estimating, your expenses. So I suggest you come up with three different budget scenarios. You may be thinking that this is a lot of work, and it is, but it will be worth it in the long run.

The first budget you make should be an incredibly optimistic budget. This is the one that you would love to see happen and that most small business owners actually believe will happen. In this budget you should put the best-case scenario, figuring in as many client sessions as you think you can handle.

The second budget should be your worst-case scenario. Imagine you have a difficult time obtaining clients and clients who miss appointments. Figure your utilities on the high end.

Finally, create a realistic budget. This budget should fall somewhere in between the previous two budgets you created. Include a realistic number of training sessions and your bills in the middle of the road. The reason for the first two budgets is to give you a clearer picture of reality when you go to create your realistic budget. Of course there is always a possibility that one of the first two budgets will turn out to be the realistic one. Hopefully it would be the first one, not the second.

Tracking Your Expenses

Formulating your budget and creating your spreadsheet of monthly bills and expenses is just the first step. Your budget is a moving target; tracking your expenses is also important. Especially at the start of your business, your budget will need to be tweaked here and there. Remember you are guessing at first. As you see the actual numbers, you will change your budget to reflect real life.

It will also be important to review your budget each month to keep abreast of where your dollars are going and if you are making a profit or are falling behind.

Profit versus Cash Flow

The difference between these two is not always understood by business owners, but get yourself ahead of the game by learning the difference. Profit and cash flow are two entirely different concepts, each with entirely different results. The concept of profit is somewhat narrow and only looks at income and expenses at a certain point in time. Cash flow, on the other hand, is more dynamic. It concentrates on the movement of money in and out of your business. More important, it shows the time at which the movement of the money takes place. You might even say the concept of cash flow is more in line with reality.

Resources for Financial Planning

Financial planning, if you do not have experience with it, is not something that you will be an expert at after reading this book. I provide you with the basics, and from there, with practice and experience, you will become efficient at it.

Here is a site I recommend for you to read or use to research questions you may have on financial planning: www.financialplan.about.com.

Cash flow statements include the inflows and outflows of cash transactions. A cash flow statement does not include things such as write-offs or equipment depreciation.

A profit (or profit and loss) statement may not always show the true picture. If you are behind on your bills, your profit statement may still show that you have made a profit, while your cash flow statement shows you exactly how much money is going in and out of your business.

How to Keep from Overspending

Overspending is a subject that cannot be stressed enough. We are all guilty of over-spending at one point or another, some of us more than others. When you see your financial statements each month, you will see where you are overspending. Your statements will help keep you in check.

Most folks don't realize just how much money they spend on a weekly basis. Think about a daily cup of coffee; that could easily add up to $600 or more a year. Or a few drinks at a bar each week could add up to over $1,000 per year. If you eat out often, you could be spending over $1,500 a year on fast food, or much higher than that if you are frequenting sit-down restaurants.

Having the discipline to keep from buying designer jeans and going out to fancy restaurants when it is clearly not in your budget may be something you will have to work on. On the other hand, if you are in the percentage of the population that is thrifty and cautious with their spending, you will have an easier time keeping your spending under control for sure.

Planning for an Economic Crisis

Your business may be moving along swimmingly; you have a steady base of clients, a new client coming along here and there, and all is looking good. You are happy with your income, and business is going well. Taking these good, steady times for granted is a mistake. Do not allow yourself to get comfortable or lazy with your clients. Always be ready for a downturn. If you get cocky or too sure of yourself, you will be one of the first ones to feel it when the economy starts to tank.

Keeping your image and reputation up is the first step to maintaining success. If you allow yourself to get lazy with your business, maybe slacking on advertising or giving a little bit less than stellar customer service, you are setting yourself up for disaster.

> **Don't Make This Mistake!**
>
> If the economy starts to look like it is turning around for the better, do not go out and start spending again as if you were a caged monkey! Hold off and continue to be conservative in your spending. The first signs of economic recovery might only be a blip, and in any event it is likely that your cash is down and you will need to spend some time building back your cash flow.

If the economy does start to suffer, conserve cash. Look at your spending habits and cut back where you can. This is when you will want to look at your variable expenses. Start making coffee at home, hold off on buying those designer jeans you wanted, cook a romantic dinner at home instead of going to a fancy restaurant, hold off on buying more equipment (unless necessary) until things start to look up again.

Creating Emotional Ties

When the economy takes a turn for the worse, and folks start losing their jobs or otherwise feeling the hurt, they look to cut costs. For most people, having a personal trainer is a luxury and a "variable cost" that they can do without—or that they think they can do without. Some people look at working out and staying fit as the most important thing they do. I know people who would (and have) cut out their cable service before canceling their gym membership. These people are the minority of the population (unfortunately for you and us). Being that the majority of people would cut out their personal trainer as a way to cut costs, it is your job to change their train of thought. Now, I am not saying that if your client is about to lose his or her house, you should persuade him or her to keep paying you as a trainer. But in cases where people are just being cautious because they hear all the terrible news about the economic crisis on the news, you need to convince them that their health and fitness are precious and something they cannot "afford" to cut back on.

Whether the economy is booming or spiraling downward, creating emotional ties is imperative to keeping your clients and can and should be done from the very first time you meet with them. This will really help you if the economy starts to decline. You have to get yourself accustomed to asking questions that have meaning and will create those emotional ties, questions that will cause your client to divulge personal issues and therefore create a tie to you and build trust.

By asking questions that most trainers do not, you will create a dialogue between you and your client that will be filled with feelings and emotions. This can create the feeling within your client that he or she needs you (which we both already know, but the key is to convince your client!).

Here are some sample questions to ask that can help build those emotional ties:

- What do you hope to achieve by training?
- How long have you been trying to lose weight?
- How have you tried to achieve your fitness goals in the past?
- Does your weight or physical condition upset you, and does it cause stress?
- Does your spouse pressure you to get more physically fit?
- If so, how does this make you feel?
- Are you completely committed to getting in shape and improving your health?
- If so, is there anything that would stand in your way or cause you to quit your commitment?

Set Yourself Apart from the Competition

You should also keep your customer service up to the highest standards no matter what the current economic situation. The better your customer service, the better position you will be in to maintain your clients.

Do something that will set you apart from the competition. A creative idea is to send a welcome kit to each new client. Imagine signing on a client for his or her first package of personal training lessons and the next day they receive a package from you. Whether they are at home or at the office, this will not only show your client that you possess a superhigh standard of customer service, but chances are your client will pick up the phone and tell their friends about you. If you send it to their place of work, there is a good chance several, maybe many, coworkers will hear about you.

The welcome kit can consist of many different items. You can send a plant or something that interests your client, making it personal, not just generic. If your client mentions that she loves ballet, you can send her a book about ballet or a pretty picture (or poster) of a ballet scene. There are many options that you can choose. The biggest benefit of the welcome kit is that it will set you apart from other personal trainers and show your client that your customer service is off the charts.

Ready for an Emergency

Aside from an economic crisis, there are other factors that may cause a dip in your cash flow. This could be your treadmill breaking down and costing hundreds of dollars to fix or having to replace it completely, which would be several thousands of dollars. If your computer crashes, it could cost hundreds of dollars to either have a computer technician rebuild it or buy a new one. There are many problems that could occur at any given time that would cost your business money that you may not have planned for.

It is easier said than done, but you should try to have a cushion in your cash flow that will allow you to handle emergencies without them being detrimental to your pocketbook. Put away some of your income each month. Ten percent is generally ideal, but I am realistic and know that that is not always going to be possible.

Nest Egg and Retirement

When owning and operating your own business, you are solely responsible for not only building a nest egg (or savings), but also for saving for retirement. It is so important that you think about retirement. You might be thinking that it is so far off, but the younger you are, the more of an advantage you have if you start now. If you are in your early twenties, putting just a few thousand dollars away each year can add up to a million dollars by the time you turn sixty-two. If you wait until you are in your early thirties, you will need to save $9,000 a year to reach a million dollars by age sixty-two. These numbers are estimates, of course; speak to a professional for accurate numbers.

Don't let this discourage you if you are in your thirties or older. Just start saving now. If $4,000 a year sounds too steep, save whatever amount you can—a few

Be Prepared

It would be a good idea to include in your budget a miscellaneous column for emergencies. On your expense sheet, include a reasonable amount, approximately $200 to $300 per month. You will not use this money every month, but if four months later an incident happens that will cost you $600, your budget will have allotted for the expense.

dollars per month is a lot better than nothing! It is surprising how it can add up over the years.

Savings

For your nest egg you can open a savings account or money market account. Money market accounts usually pay higher interest, but usually have a minimum balance to maintain, which may be too high for you at first. Talk to a business banker or investment banker to get the best advice on what you should open for your own particular situation.

Once you have some money saved, you might want to look at opening a certificate of deposit (CD). Just make sure you won't need to dip into the money, because with a CD there is a penalty for withdrawing funds prior to the maturity date.

Retirement

Saving for retirement is serious business, which is why I recommend getting advice from a professional. If you do not know anyone who can direct you, start at your bank and ask whom to speak to regarding retirement plans.

A popular retirement plan is the Individual Retirement Account (IRA). There are several IRAs to choose from; your banker can advise you on the best option for your situation.

In addition to opening an IRA, you can find out about opening a brokerage account. While this may sound like a scary proposition, with the correct guidance from your investment banker, it could be a good route for you to take.

Basically, having a brokerage account means you are investing in the stock market. Most banks make this easy. You deposit your savings into your money market account and then the broker transfers the money into the brokerage account. Yes, the stock market goes up and down, but many people have become quite wealthy (or filthy rich) from investing in stocks, so it is certainly worth looking into.

07

Financial Management

Opening a Business Account

When running a business, it's a good idea to open a business checking account. More than likely you have a personal bank account already, so you might have a relationship with your bank. If so, speak with a representative at the bank who can explain all the options, fees, and other information you need to make a decision. The fees on a business checking account can add up, though, so it's a good idea to shop around at several banks to compare their fees and options.

To open a business account, you will need to have several things in order:

- Your Tax ID Number or Employee Identification Number
- Business paperwork (you business license)
- Your driver's license or passport
- Your Social Security number

Your business account will be used to deposit all of your income and pay all of your bills. Having a business account makes it clear as to what money is coming in and out of your business. If you have multiple accounts, or use your personal account also, it can become unorganized and be nearly impossible to figure out your taxes.

Business Credit Card

The best option when it comes to getting a business credit card is to have your business checking account card serve this purpose. Most banks, if not all, offer a business checking account card that has a Visa or MasterCard logo on it.

Let me explain. You will be making regular business purchases once your business is up and running. You may buy cleaning supplies, additional equipment, and so on. It is best to make all of these purchases on one business card. This way it is easy to track exactly where your money is going.

The reason I say your business checking account card is the best option is because it is not a credit card. The money will come directly out of your business checking account. This is the best way to keep yourself from racking up unnecessary debt. However, I know this may not always be feasible, and that is why I said a business checking account card is your "best option." It is important, however, that you avoid going into overdraft. I will discuss this more in chapter 8.

Applying for a Loan

You need to figure out how much money you have and how much money you need. I have reviewed expenses, cost of equipment, start-up costs, and so on. So you should have a pretty good idea of how much money you will realistically need to get your business going.

If you are short only a few thousand dollars (up to $8,000 or $9,000), you may be able to get a credit card to make up this difference. If you do, be careful! Do not allow yourself to fall into the rut of keeping your balance at the maximum. You should always pay more than the minimum balance due, and once you have made your initial purchases, you should not carry the card around in your wallet. Doing so only makes it too much of a temptation. Instead, put it away in a safe place to be used only for emergencies (a Gucci handbag is *not* an emergency!). Only paying the minimum balance due each month will keep your balance high, instead of decreasing it each month. It is not always easy to pay more than the minimum due, but try to pay as much as you can each month without hurting your checking account.

SBA Loan

SBA stands for Small Business Administration. SBA exists to help small businesses start, build, and grow.

An SBA loan is a good option for you if you need a significant amount of capital to get your business started. Take a look at the official Web site for SBA loans, www .sba.gov/aboutsba/index.html, or visit your local bank for more information.

Client Payment Schedule

When it comes to collecting payment from clients, you should have policies set in place. Too often small business owners fall into the rut of giving their clients too much leeway. This can end up leaving your pockets empty!

Importance of Enforcing Payment Policies

If you say to your clients, "It's okay, pay me next time," or if a client says to you, "I want to start training twice a week, but I won't have the money until next month," this is a recipe for financial disaster. You have to stand your ground. Most clients will mean well when they say they will pay you next time; however, next time turns into next week, which can turn into next month. Before you know it, you've trained someone several times, and then they cancel and you never got paid!

It is difficult to say no to people. For one, you worry about losing a client. But this is an unfounded fear. If a client is committed to training with you, he or she will be okay with paying you on time. Second, it is in a lot of people's nature to want to

---

Another Way to Look at It

So you feel shy about saying no to your clients; you want to make them happy. But you are a businessperson, you are in business to make a living and run a respectable show.

If you went into a clothing store to buy a pair of jeans and said to the salesperson, "I really need these jeans for a party I have tonight, but I won't be able to pay you until next week," what do you think would happen? Do you really think the salesperson would let you take the jeans without paying? *No!*

make clients happy. But allowing clients to pay you late only lessens the credibility of your business and the respect you will earn and deserve.

Credit Cards: The Good, the Bad, and the Options!

Should you or should you not accept credit cards? There are several options to consider when making this decision.

The Good

Accepting credit cards as payment adds convenience for your clients. These days, most folks do not carry a lot of cash on them or a checkbook. You can easily say, "Cash or check only," but by accepting credit cards you will add to your credibility as a professional businessperson and show your clients that you are flexible.

The Bad

With accepting credit cards come fees. Every time you process a transaction, you are charged a fee by your merchant. These fees can vary, so shop around. If you accept credit cards, you can decide to accept Visa and MasterCard only if you choose. American Express charges its own set of fees, most often higher than Visa and MasterCard. Accepting American Express may not be such a bad idea, because the majority of clients will use Visa or MasterCard. Fees vary and can be anywhere from 1 percent (very low end) to close to 3 percent of the transaction amount. What's more, there are fees on top of the percentage, so be cautious and thorough when you shop around.

Many companies have a laundry list of fees; you want to know what these are, so be sure to ask (some companies may conveniently leave these very important details out). These additional fees may include (but are not limited to):

- If the card is not present at the time of processing—meaning you manually enter the card number instead of swiping it—the fee can be substantially higher.
- Chargeback is when your client's bank orders a reversal of the charge to the client's card. This is not at all good, as the fees associated with chargeback can be astronomical—plus you are not getting paid!
- If a client uses a corporate card, the bank tends to charge what may be referred to as a "commercial rate" for transactions with that card.

You Have Options

It does not have to be cut-and-dry when it comes to accepting credit cards. You can implement a policy to charge a slightly higher price if your client wants to pay with a credit card. This way the fees do not directly affect your bottom line.

Ordering Your Equipment

I have discussed equipment at length—what kind to buy, how much it may cost, where to put it, and so on. So now it's time to order that equipment. At this point you should have a list of equipment you would like to buy. And with your finances and floor plan in place, it is now time to place your order for equipment.

When deciding on equipment purchases, factor in: size/space, price, and versatility (equipment that allows you to perform multiple exercises).

08

Taxes and Record Keeping

Keeping Your Financial Records Organized

Keeping your financial records organized is a very important aspect of your business, so do yourself a big favor and keep your financials organized from the very beginning. If you keep on track from the get-go, you will thank yourself later—especially when tax time rolls around!

As mentioned in the previous chapter, using *one* credit card, or your business checking account, for all your business-related purchases is a great way to keep organized. With all your purchases on one card, you have one statement and can easily enter each transaction into your financial software, making record keeping simple!

I realize, however, that this is not always possible. If you decide to use multiple credit cards, keep up with your records. Ideally, the credit cards you use for your business should be strictly for business purchases, not personal also. If you are mixing business and personal, I suggest that when you get your statements, you highlight the business expenses first, before filing them away.

Software

Financial software allows you to track expenses and run reports such as profit and loss statements. It will definitely be your friend come tax time! If you use your software to keep your records organized and up-to-date, your life will be a lot easier in a lot of ways, or at least you'll avoid potential headaches and time-consuming "clean-up" later on.

There are so many options when it comes to financial software. If you are already familiar with one type, stick with it, as long as it fulfills your business needs. If you do not know where to begin, ask other small business owners. I personally prefer Quickbooks; it is very user-friendly. If you do not have experience with financial software, you will definitely appreciate one that is user-friendly. However, there are many options, so ask around and do some research online to help you make your decision.

Keep Receipts Organized

Receipts can be like a pesky ant problem! They seem to keep coming and can really create mayhem. If you keep up with your receipts, however, you will have it all under control and will never have to face the "hill" of papers.

To keep receipts organized use a simple filing system. You can use file pockets, or "file wallets," as these are great for keeping smaller papers such as receipts. You can label each pocket to categorize your receipts according to each type of expense from your monthly expense report and every year start a new one.

You can also use your regular filing cabinet to store your receipts, but receipts are so small that you might find smaller file pockets make organizing (and then finding) receipts easier.

Tracking Clients' Payments

Get in the habit from the very beginning of tracking your clients' payments. You may not think so now, but it is easy to lose track of payments. One way to stay organized is to create a simple form (see example on the next page), for each individual client. You can then easily track when each session occurs and when it is paid.

Keeping up with this simple system will allow you to make sure your clients' payments are up-to-date, and you will not have to worry or stress about cash flow. Organized systems will only improve the quality of your business and the ease with which you sail through the paperwork.

Should You Hire a Bookkeeper?

Hiring a bookkeeper may be beneficial to your business. If you have experience in keeping your financials in order, and feel comfortable doing it, then maybe you will hold off until you feel you need some assistance.

If you feel incompetent at keeping your books, then hire a bookkeeper. You can do this right when you start your business. It is always a good idea to know what is going on with your finances, so I recommend having your bookkeeper teach you how to handle your books yourself. If you do not feel comfortable with all the aspects of bookkeeping after your "tutorial," then you may want to consider partial

Laura's Studio

Name_____ #_____

Personal Training Log

Date	Sessions	Workout Log

involvement. I personally enter all my transactions into Quickbooks and pay the bills. My bookkeeper then comes once a month to reconcile the month and create statements. This system works well for me.

If you are unsure if you are doing things absolutely perfectly, call for help! Contact a bookkeeper to look over your books and make sure you are handling them. You do not want to risk messing this up.

Know What Your Deductions Are

When you purchase something, you will need to know if it qualifies as a business expense (other words you may come across for *expense* are *deduction* and *write-off*). You should be able to make this decision without batting an eyelash after a short time in business. For example, if you have a land-line telephone that is strictly for your business office, that is a business expense. If you purchase ink for your office printer, that is a business expense. If you purchase a new choo-choo train for your child, this is *not* a business expense.

Tax Time

Doing the taxes is not something most people look forward to. However, as you know, it must be done! You will be ahead of the game if you follow my advice and stay organized with your financials throughout the year.

Hiring a CPA (Certified Public Accountant)

Hiring a CPA can be a good idea for a small business owner. A CPA can offer assurance that your taxes are done correctly. After all, this is not something you want to take lightly or make mistakes on.

A CPA can guide you throughout the year, should you have questions that neither you nor your bookkeeper (should you choose to have one) are able to answer. And while you may be thinking that you will save money if you do not hire a CPA, this is not always the case. An experienced and smart CPA may actually save you money in the long run.

Be sure to do some research before hiring a CPA, however. Don't just flip open the yellow pages, point your finger at the page, and call the first CPA you land on. Speak to fellow small business owners and visit the Web sites of CPAs in your area. You will want to make sure the CPA you choose is savvy in the areas that you need him or her to be.

Deadlines for Corporate Taxes

I don't think there is anyone out there who doesn't cringe when he or she hears the date April 15. Well, you can rest easy, because this is *not* your date (at least not for your business)! The deadline for corporate tax returns is March 15. Yes, a month earlier—for all of you procrastinators out there, I am sorry to be the bearer of bad news. However, if you take my advice and stay organized, this should be a piece of cake!

More than likely your CPA will advise and set you up to pay estimated taxes quarterly. This is always a good idea to keep you from having a big shock to your pocket come March 15!

Don't panic if you are absolutely unable to "get it together" by March 15; your CPA can file for an extension to September 15. A good CPA can further explain all these details.

09 Legal and Ethical Issues

Insurance

When it comes to insurance, you do not want to play a guessing game. I went directly to an expert to make sure I gave you thorough and precise information. Ken Reinsig of the Association Insurance Group located in Kennesaw, Georgia, recommends the following:

> Most homeowner's insurance policies exclude coverage for business property and liability for home-based commercial businesses. Since every personal lines (homeowner's) insurance company looks at home-based businesses a little differently, your first course of action is to contact the agent who provides your homeowner's insurance to see if your personal training business would be covered under your homeowner's insurance or if adding your business can be achieved by paying an additional premium.

Chances are, your personal training business will not be covered under your homeowner's policy. If this is the case, there are three types of insurance you should consider:

1. Property insurance to cover your equipment, fixtures, improvements, and loss of income protection.
2. General liability insurance to cover premises-related injuries such as slips and falls and malfunctioning equipment.
3. Professional liability to cover you for injuries sustained by your clients as a result of your training techniques and/or exercise and nutritional advice.

If you want complete coverage for all three areas, then you would purchase a package policy that is usually designed for commercial personal training studios. Instead of leasing space from a commercial building owner, you are, in essence, leasing space from yourself as the property owner. Whether there is an actual contract or lease in place is not necessarily important. What is important is that there is an exclusion under the homeowner's policy that triggers the need to have a standalone policy to protect your training business.

Most trainers are not concerned with insuring business property, improvements, or loss of income protection. Usually the equipment investment in a home training business is not significant enough to worry about, and most property policies have a $1,000 deductible anyway. In other words, trainers are usually not concerned with this exposure to loss. What trainers *are* concerned about is exposure to liability and professional liability.

Legalities of Signage

If you would like to hang a sign outside of your home, you will first have to make sure that it is legal to do so. Some neighborhoods or homeowner associations have rules and regulations concerning business advertising on a residential property. There may be rules you have to follow, or perhaps you cannot hang anything at all. You want to find all of this out before you waste money on getting a sign made that you then cannot use. (Refer back to chapter 2 on how to go about checking on this.)

Know Your Boundaries

As a personal trainer you should always keep up with your certifications. Clients will ask you for all kinds of advice, assuming you are an expert in additional fields such as nutrition and supplements. Think before you speak. Unless you are certified in nutrition, you should not give direct advice; suggestions are okay, but make it clear you are not certified.

It would be a good idea to know a reputable nutritionist or two whom you can refer your clients to. This will help you to keep your clients, rather than have them leave you for a trainer/nutritionist.

Prescribing versus Recommending

You may have clients, and I am sure you will, who will have unhealthy or even downright terrible eating habits. This of course is not good for anyone, and you will not want to ignore it. If your client is walking in your studio with a milkshake from McDonald's . . . that would be something to address!

However, it is bound to happen that some of your clients will ask you and expect you to be an expert on nutrition and maybe even supplements. Sitting down and writing out a diet for your client is not something you should be doing. Nor should you be "prescribing" supplements. Sure, you can "recommend" supplements and give pointers on nutrition, but unless you are a certified nutritionist, you should be pretty vague with suggestions.

If nutrition is something that interests you, you might consider becoming a certified nutritionist. This would be a great way to offer your clients an additional benefit of having you as a trainer, and it would be an additional source of income.

Steer Clear of Sexual Harassment

While it is unfortunate, sexual harassment is a real possibility that you must seriously keep in mind. Whether you are a man or a woman, as a personal trainer you are at risk of being blamed for sexual harassment or falling victim to it. And when your business is in your home, you really open yourself up to it. After all, most often your training sessions will be between you and your client alone in your studio. Not to scare you, but this situation does put you at a certain amount of risk.

Very often, innocent conversation between two people can be misread as sexual harassment. You should always keep yourself in check in your conduct with your clients. It is easy to create casual flirting without even realizing it. Some people have a natural way about them that makes it seem as if they are flirting, even when they do not mean to.

Use your radar and common sense when accepting new clients. Ask yourself:

- Do I have mutual friends with this person?
- How did they hear about me?
- Has this person lived in the area for a long time?

If your potential new client is a complete stranger, you might want to consider meeting for the first time in a public place. Maybe set up a meeting as a preassessment. You can see if you are comfortable with the person. Often our instincts let us know if a person makes us feel uncomfortable. Trust your gut instinct.

Should you decide to turn down a potential client for any reason, choose your words wisely. If they have a certain limitation, you can say that you are not knowledgeable in their area of need. You might also ask them what time they are available, and make it turn out that your schedules are conflicting. These are just a couple of examples, but each situation will be different. Your goal will be to not offend anyone.

Protect Your Reputation

It is very important to protect your reputation. Building a good reputation and keeping it is a lot of work, but it will make a world of difference to your success.

Having your own business is a great responsibility; you and you alone are responsible for how your community perceives you. From the very beginning, before your business is even started, you should start molding your reputation. We all have bad days, but you represent your business, so always keep that in mind when you are out in public.

Provide Consistent Service

Your level of service should be consistent. If you train a client and are energetic and peppy one session but then cranky and sluggish the next, your client will likely remember and talk about your down day. This is simply human nature—to remember the negative and dismiss the positive. You want your clients to always have a good impression of you so that there will be no question, no hesitance, no reason for them to say anything negative about you at all.

It is imperative to be consistently professional. Always remember that each client and each session is as important as the next if you want to uphold the shining reputation you've worked so hard to achieve!

Should You Train to Work with the Physically Challenged?

There are a couple of reasons why you might want to consider getting trained to work with people who are physically challenged.

For one, an existing client may get into an accident, or for some other reason become physically impaired. This client may then need you more than ever. Another reason is if business is growing slowly, this would be a whole new avenue of potential clients. You can visit hospitals and rehab centers to see if you can recruit clients that way.

Now, I am not saying to "wing" this. Training people with physical impairments or challenges should not be taken lightly. Do not attempt to accept such clients unless you have undergone proper and thorough training and feel 100 percent confident that you are knowledgeable enough to make a positive difference in their lives.

The Ethics of Training Clients from Past Jobs

If you are already a personal trainer and work out of a local gym, whether you are an employee or independent trainer, you will be dealing with the ethical issue of having your clients from the gym follow you to your home studio.

Of course, if your clients do not want to follow you, you should think about why. But chances are, you are a very good (or great) personal trainer and your clients are going to want to continue to train with you. When that is the case, I suggest two ways to go about handling the situation. First, you can continue to train your existing clients out of the gym. Do not solicit or suggest that they come to your studio to train, but do tell them that you are starting your home business. They may on their own decide to move to your studio. This is always tough, though, because the gym owner is not going to be happy with you "taking" business from his or her establishment. However, in some instances you will not be able to control that. If your client wants to train out of your house instead of the gym, it won't help anyone for you to say no—not you, your client, or the gym owner.

You might want to consider keeping a relationship with the gym. Be prepared to have some clients who will much prefer the atmosphere and diversity of working out in a gym setting rather than in your studio. There is nothing wrong with still training some clients out of the gym. You might have been thinking that once you had your home studio, that's it. But keep your mind and possibilities open. You can do both, if that is what makes sense for you.

Get That Waiver and Release Signed

Your clients can get injured in your studio, whether they drop a fifty-pound dumbbell on their foot or trip over a piece of equipment—anything can happen.

But you can protect yourself by having your clients—each and every one of them—sign a waiver and release form. It's also important to keep a neat and tidy studio.

I cannot stress enough how important it is to have clients sign a waiver and release form. It takes just a few minutes to give them the form and have them read it and sign it. The form should be printed on two-part NCR (two-part "carbonless" paper). Keep the original (top) copy in the client's file and give him or her the other copy. Having this signed form can help protect you against lawsuits. And lawsuits are often a small business owner's biggest fear. Of course you will have insurance, but having claims filed against you can increase your insurance costs exorbitantly. So keep yourself protected.

To help avoid some accidents in the first place, do not leave accessories or other equipment lying around. Try to create an easy flow throughout the studio, without a lot of obstacles in the way.

Knowing When to Use a Medical Release Form

You may have clients who immediately raise a red flag; they may (and should when you conduct their assessment) come out and tell you that they have a heart condition, experience seizures, have had a stroke in the past, or are recovering from a serious illness. In these cases, the red flag has been raised and you should ask them to obtain a medical release form from their doctor.

Waiver and Release

I (buyer, each member, and all guests) am fourteen years of age or older and agree that if I engage in any physical activity or use any equipment on the premises, I do so at my own risk. This includes, without limitation, my use of the locker room, studios, gym facilities, or any equipment in the club, and my participation in any activity, class, program, personal training, or instruction. I agree that I am voluntarily participating in these activities and using these facilities and premises and assume all risk of injury, illness, damage, or loss to me or my property. I agree on behalf of myself (and my personal representatives, successors, and assigns) to release and discharge Laura's Studio (any Laura's Studio affiliates, employees, agents, representatives, successors, and assigns) from any and all claims or causes of action (known or unknown) arising out of Laura's Studio's negligence. This waiver and release of liability includes, without limitation, injuries that may occur as a result of (a) my use of any exercise equipment or facilities that may malfunction or break, (b) any improper maintenance of any exercise equipment or facility, (c) any negligent instruction or supervision, and (d) my slipping and falling while in the health club or on the premises. I acknowledge that I have read this waiver and release and fully understand that it is a release of liability. In consideration of being able to use the facilities and equipment at Laura's Studio, which consideration is in addition to the dues I agree to pay under this agreement, I am waiving any current or future right that I may have to bring legal action to assert a claim against Laura's Studio for both my negligence and that of Laura's Studio. There are definite risks associated with the use of exercise equipment that cannot be avoided. In consideration of being permitted to use the facilities and equipment of Laura's Studio, the member, guest, and personal representatives, heirs, and next of kin, hereby releases, waives, discharges, and covenants not to sue Laura's Studio, its officers, directors, shareholders, or any employees, or otherwise while the member, guest is using the facility and/or equipment of Laura's Studio.

There will be times, however, when a client appears perfectly healthy and discloses no information that would give you reason for concern. Set a guideline for yourself to follow when it comes to having "healthy clients" get a medical release signed.

Client Cancellation Policy

It is a good idea to protect your income with a cancellation policy. Do not feel that it is difficult to enforce. I know that often a trainer and client become friends, and that is when enforcing a cancellation policy can be sticky. But just like your payment policy, you should enforce your cancellation policy as well.

I am not saying that there will not be circumstances that would call for bending the rules; there will always be gray areas. For instance, your client might have a family emergency, such as their child being rushed to the hospital or something terrible like that. In these cases you should waive your policy, just out of human decency. But to protect yourself against "flaky" clients, you should have and enforce a cancellation policy.

An common policy is a twenty-four-hour cancellation policy, whereby if the client does not give twenty-four hours' notice that he or she cannot keep the appointment, he or she will be charged the session or half the session price.

The Importance of Having an Attorney

A good business attorney can provide you with vital assistance in almost every facet of your business, from basic zoning compliance, trademark issues, and formal business incorporation, to lawsuits and liability.

You may be thinking, "I don't need a lawyer until I have a reason to hire one." Well, that may be the way most business owners think, always trying to save a buck, but you are reading this book because you want to open your business with the greatest possible chance at success. If you wait until you run into a problem—for example, you receive a summons from the chief of police—it is too late. Your lawyer could have helped you avoid getting into trouble in the first place. Now it is just a matter of how much you have to pay the court. By this point, a lawyer will most likely not be able to help much; the damage is already done.

10 Marketing Your Business

Advertising and Marketing Objectives

Every business must engage in advertising and marketing in order to build its business. Storefront businesses have an advantage—visibility. They have foot traffic, which creates walk-ins, which in turn are potential customers. Storefront businesses pay big rents and overhead for this visibility and foot traffic. You are saving a bundle by opening your business out of your home, so spend some of that money you're saving on advertising and get your name out there!

The objective of marketing is to build a successful business. There is an abundance of choices when it comes to marketing your business. In this chapter, I will go over several choices, but keep in mind that this is not all of them. You may come up with your own creative ideas, or you may come across different methods other businesses are using. It is beneficial to try different venues and methods. That way, you target a wider population, and you won't be limiting yourself to the same group of people each time you advertise.

With all the talk about pricey and not-so-pricey marketing ideas in this chapter, keep in mind that advertising alone will not make you successful. A healthy and balanced combination of advertising and marketing, along with great—no, extraordinary—customer service will put you on the road to success and keep you there. There is no room for slacking or laziness when it comes to the success of your business. Keep up a smart marketing strategy and always provide the best customer service possible, and you won't leave any room for failure.

Business Cards

Business cards are a necessity and a very inexpensive way to market your business. Whenever you are out in your community, you meet and talk to people all the time. Maybe you are out at a restaurant and strike up a conversation with the hostess, or while you are in the supermarket you might start talking to the guy next to you squeezing the melons . . . no matter where you are, conversations start all the time. (Start to take notice; you'll be surprised how many people you actually talk to during the course of any given day.)

Your business cards should be printed professionally, unless you have a very good printer. Business cards that are printed on a normal home printer look like they have been printed at home, and that looks unprofessional. The cost for professionally printed business cards varies from $25 to $75 for five hundred to one thousand cards. It is a small price to pay for quality.

Your business cards should consist of your logo and all your contact information, including your name, phone number(s), e-mail address, and Web site. You can choose to have your address printed on the business cards or not. You may choose not to as a safety precaution, as you might hand out your business cards pretty freely, post them on bulletin boards, or perhaps leave a handful at a local business establishment (for their customers to take). You may want to opt to have folks call you or contact you via your e-mail or Web site before you give out your address.

The design of your business cards can be as simple or as intricate as you like. There is no right or wrong look, but you want your card to stand out or "pop" just

Real-Life Story

When choosing your business cards, the printer (or designer, if you use one) may suggest glossy paper. I highly suggest that you do *not* use glossy paper, for one main reason: You cannot write on it. Often when a person gets a business card, he or she wants to jot down a note or another phone number on the card. The trouble is, you cannot write on glossy paper. What's more, glossy paper costs more, so it really is not a good choice.

I ordered glossy business cards once, because I had a graphic designer who wanted to make all sorts of decisions (this was short-lived). I ended up with one thousand business cards that I eventually threw into the garbage. So basically I spent double the money, because I ordered a whole new batch of cards on matte paper. I also had to deal with the aggravation that came with it.

enough that it grabs people's attention. On the other hand, you don't want it to pop so much that it causes folks to get dizzy when they look at it. One idea is to have a colored background, such as yellow, with black lettering. This would keep costs down but still grab attention. Normally printers charge more for more than one color print, so expect to pay more if you have red and blue ink or whatever other combination you might choose.

Yellow Page Ads

Advertising in the yellow pages is a very traditional form of advertising. But with the Internet, it is becoming less popular. However, if you are listed in the yellow pages, your listing will show up on the Internet listings as well (double-check this when you place the order).

People still do use the phone book or yellow pages when they are looking for something in particular, especially when it has to do with a local business or service such as yours. Advertising in the yellow pages does not have to cost a whole lot. You can do a "line ad" or opt for a small ad that will draw more attention to your business.

If you do a yellow pages ad, include points that will create interest, such as:

- One-on-One Training with a Certified Personal Trainer
- Look Great, Feel Great
- Improve Your Health, Live Longer
- Packages Available for Discounted Rates

Of course, these are just some examples of what you might want to put in your ad. Including words or phrases that may grab people's attention is what your goal should be. You want your ad to cause people to call you and ultimately become your client. After all, if you are going to spend the money to place the ad, make it "pop," make it money well spent.

Networking

You hear the word *networking* all the time. It has become very common in everyday conversation. That's because networking is one of the single most important ways to market your business, and most often it comes at a small price!

Networking is a way to share your business, information, and services with people who are interested in your field or have a common interest. There are many ways for you to network your home-based personal trainer business.

Local Gyms

You might be thinking, "What? Network at my local gym? They are my competition!" Think again: They might be your competition, but you can be witty and use them to your advantage. Most often a good businessperson is always looking for ways to increase his or her revenue, build business, and provide as many options to customers as possible. This is where you come in; you can offer the local gym an opportunity to offer their customers a broader range of possibilities and choices when it comes to reaching their health and fitness goals.

So how do you network with your local gym? Chances are you might already know the manager or owner of the gym. But even if you don't, approach the owner or manager and discuss the possibility of the gym offering your services to train clients out of your home (or in the gym) in return for a percentage of your fee. Yes, you will make less money on the hour, but think of the possibilities in getting new clients. Your base of clients would have the potential to grow quite significantly (depending of course on the size and volume of the gym).

Massage Therapists

Visit the massage therapists in your area. This is a nice opportunity for you to grow your business at no cost and to help a peer grow their business as well.

Your goal here would be to set up an agreement by which you would refer each other to your own existing clients. You could have the massage therapist's business cards or small brochures in your studio and your paraphernalia in the massage therapist's office. In addition to displaying marketing materials, the power of suggestion is a wonderful thing. After all, who doesn't enjoy getting a massage?

Sports Doctors

Like massage therapists, sports doctors can be great allies to have! A sports doctor's patients will most likely be active people who are also into fitness. That is where you come in. By networking and forming a partnership with one or more local sports doctors, you will open up the possibilities for both of your businesses to grow.

Health Food Stores

Another great avenue for potential networking is health food stores. Often folks who work out also like to eat healthy; it just seems to go hand in hand. So getting acquainted with health food store owners and/or managers is a good opportunity for you to do some good networking.

Cross-Marketing

Cross-marketing is a great way to create business and also cut costs on promotional materials. With cross-marketing you pair up with another business (perhaps the health food store) and do a cross-promotion—you create a coupon or flyer that offers a "special" or "discount."

One example of cross-marketing might be a flyer that reads, "Bring in your receipt from a $50 purchase at ABC Health Food Store and get your first training session free." And on the other half of the flyer it might say, "Clients of Laura Augenti, personal trainer, get 10 percent off their next purchase at ABC Health Food Store." This tactic cuts the cost of printed materials, because you share the expense with the health food store.

Another example of cross-marketing is to have your coupons in the health food store; maybe they give one to each customer with their receipt, and you give your clients a coupon from the health food store.

Health and Wellness Fairs

Health and wellness fairs are a great way for you to get exposure. Check your local newspapers, community center, chamber of commerce, YMCA, and so on to keep informed of such events. When you find a fair, you can either set up a booth or just attend the event and network. If you can set up a booth, that would be a great opportunity for you to meet potential clients and hand out your marketing and advertising materials. Having a booth usually costs money, however, so you will have to decide if the potential for new business is worth the cost.

Special Issues

Some papers will have special issues that they print every so often throughout the year. The local paper on Maui, the *Maui Weekly,* has special issues such as "Get Fit for Summer" and special health and fitness issues. These are perfect examples of issues you'd want to advertise in.

Local Newspapers

Trial and error will teach you if newspaper ads will work for you. A local newspaper that lists local stores, events, and any information regarding your community would be your best bet for newspaper advertising.

I suggest trying an ad and putting something in it that will allow you to track how much traffic you get from it. For instance, have the ad offer something to clients, such as a percentage discount off training session/s with mention of the ad. If you don't get much response, try again in a couple of weeks with a different ad, maybe with an even better discount or offer.

Free Advertising!

A great way to get *free* advertising is to contact your local paper and say that you want them to do a "press release" about you. In order for the paper to agree to do a press release, you should do something worthy of getting in the newspaper! Maybe you trained a celebrity or helped out underprivileged people in some way.

Word of Mouth

Never underestimate the power of word of mouth, for it may be your most valuable marketing tool. And the best part is that it's free! Building a stellar reputation, and keeping it up, will pay off in the end—literally. Your clients will tell friends, and they will tell friends, and so on and so on.

If you make a positive impression on someone and are influencing his or her life in a good way, he or she is bound to tell family and friends how you have improved

Real-Life Story

When you are in the fitness industry, there is no higher honor than to have the "Governator" use your services! No, I doubt that Arnold Schwarzenegger will be calling you to train him, but this is just an example. Stars use personal trainers all the time.

While vacationing on Maui in 2007, Governor Schwarzenegger, along with Ralf Moeller ("Conan the Adventurer"), came into my Powerhouse Gym and worked out. This was very exciting, not to mention great publicity for the gym. And we were able to get a press release from this.

his or her quality of life. This is the best recognition you can achieve and a great way to acquire new clients.

Merchants in a Related Field

In addition to networking, there are other ways to use local merchants to grow your business. Seek out businesses that are somewhat related to fitness, such as sports equipment or sports apparel stores. Often the people who work at these stores are somewhat into health and fitness.

Speak to the managers or owners of these local establishments and offer them and their employees a small discount on personal training with you. Or perhaps you can work out a trade that would be beneficial to both of you.

Trades can be a great way to do business—sometimes. Of course you need to make money to live, but once in a while, a trade can really be beneficial to both parties involved. If you are not familiar with what a trade is, it is when you exchange your service (or product) with another person's/business's service (or product).

Trades are popular in small-town environments, along the lines of the "old days" when they used to "barter." If you ever watched *Little House on the Prairie,* you know what I mean.

Real-Life Story

Living on Maui for four years, you learn that trades are a way of life. There were many instances where I traded with other businesses to get services/goods that I would purchase anyway. So, in exchange for a little of my time, I would get stuff for free.

One example of a trade I have done is with my graphic designer. In exchange for use of my facility, she did not charge me for designing my promotional ads. A second example of a trade that I have done is for radio advertising. The radio jockey received free training in exchange (or trade) for radio air time for my business. Trading like this will likely not work in large cities and for major radio stations, but in small towns, these trades are more easily worked out.

You can try to do trades with massage therapists, chiropractors, and any other service or product you might be interested in.

Volunteering

Volunteering for a charity or nonprofit organization can be very rewarding in more ways than one. By volunteering your time, you get noticed in the community as a "do-gooder," or "good Samaritan," if you will. Volunteering goes a long way in building your reputation.

There are so many opportunities to volunteer. If you are unsure where to begin, check with your local church or the American Red Cross. Choose something that you are passionate about. If you have a soft spot for children, do something to help children. Perhaps there is a Big Brothers, Big Sisters program or an after-school teen center in your community that needs volunteers. Whatever your passion or interest, there is sure to be a volunteer opportunity.

Auctions and Fund-Raisers

If you are like me, you like to plan and get involved in events—especially charity events. Charities and fund-raisers are a great way to accomplish two things that will make you feel good and help others.

First, you donate your service to the event—maybe a gift certificate for personal training sessions—with the hope that you will win over the person who gets the free sessions and he or she will eventually become a paying client. Second, you do

Real-Life Story

I was a member of the Business Volunteer Council in Danbury, Connecticut, from approximately 1999 to 2001. We did volunteer and charity work for different charities in the town.

One specific charity that I participated in two years in a row was the Dress for Success program. This program helped children from underprivileged families get school supplies and clothes so they could go to school and get the education they deserved.

While this volunteering helped my career, it more importantly helped kids by putting a smile on their faces, giving them supplies and clothes, and making their lives a little better. That was priceless!

something good for the cause. If it is an auction or fund-raiser, chances are it benefits a worthy cause. This is a win-win situation!

Tourism

This may not apply to you, but if you live in an area that has high tourism, or moder-
ate tourism, you may want to use that as a target for business.

Yes, folks on vacation do still work out and even want a trainer while on vacation. This is not the majority of vacationers, but you would be surprised at how many

people out there would use a trainer while on vacation. When folks use a trainer at home, they often want to do something to keep up their fitness level when they travel. So these people often will look for a trainer when the travel, especially if they travel often.

Hotel Concierge

The concierge at the hotels in your area can be your best friends! Visit each hotel (you may want to call ahead for an appointment) and meet with the concierge, the concierge manager, or perhaps someone in the human resources department—meet with whomever it is that would potentially be willing to referr clients to you. Your goal is to make a deal with this person so that he or she will refer their guests to you. When a tourist wants to find a personal trainer, whom are they going to ask? They'll ask the hotel concierge—that is what they are there for after all!

Tracking Your Advertising Dollars

It's all well and good to advertise, use creative marketing tools, and get your name out there in your community as much as possible. But you can end up wasting hundreds or thousands of dollars every year if you don't track which advertising venues are working and which are sucking your bank account dry.

Create a chart, listing all of the possible ways that someone could have found you. List every place you have advertised, such as newspapers, community bulletin boards, and so on. Having a chart will keep all the guessing out of the equation. Then, whenever you get an inquiry, however it arises, ask the person how he or she heard about you. Then mark it down on your chart.

Create this chart from the very beginning, before you open your business, and then continue to keep it going throughout the life of your business. Trends change; the marketing techniques that work for you now may not work next year or in five years. What is your best advertising venue at one point may eventually become your worst.

Consistency Counts

If you're thinking you will spend money on advertising and marketing in the beginning and then stop, you should reconsider this strategy. Maintaining your advertising is crucial. Yes, you may spend more on advertising and marketing in the beginning, but you should never stop completely. Keeping your business out there in your community says that your business is legitimate. Most people will think that a business that is seen and heard around town is a reputable one. Advertising is a way to build trust and earn respect for your business.

Keeping up consistent advertising also portrays to your community that you care about your business. This can go a long way when potential clients are deciding on a personal trainer.

Real-Life Story

Before I opened the Powerhouse Gym on Maui, I used to think that one ad here and there would be enough—boy was I wrong. But then one person, one salesperson named Johnny Absalom, the sales representative from the local radio station, taught me that consistency is imperative to successful advertising.

I remember when Johnny first walked into my presales office. At first I looked at him as one of those "annoying" (sorry, Johnny) salespeople coming to try to get me to spend my advertising dollars with him. And of course that is partly true—I mean, the guy has got to eat, no? But there was something about Johnny that caused me to give him a chance to "sell" me on advertising on his radio station. He seemed sincere, and it ended up that he was. I listened, half heartedly, to what he had to say. He kept telling me that consistency was so important to the success of the ad. I kept telling him that I didn't want to spend all that money on advertising every month. I was trying to pinch pennies, which is not always the best idea when it comes to advertising (be savvy and spend where it works).

I ended up taking Johnny's advice and placed a one-minute commercial on his radio station. I ended up with a radio commercial several times a day, four days a week, every week from that moment forward. (I believe that the gym, which I no longer own, still advertises with Johnny!) After a while, the relationship I built with Johnny was a close friendship, and that was a good thing. It was apparent then that there was more to the sale than just cash; he became genuinely interested in the success of the gym.

People in the community were always saying to us, "I heard your ad again," or "Nice commercial; I like this one." Because we kept the ads running constantly, we did not use the same one all the time; that would bore anyone to tears. We changed the commercial approximately once a month, basing it on a membership special or integrating it with the current season or holiday. That way the public knew we were out there, but did not fall asleep listening to the same old ad over and over again. The results from our consistent advertising proved it to be worthwhile.

You may not be using radio advertising, as it can be quite expensive for a home-based business budget. However, this is just an example of how consistent advertising can pay off. You can choose to apply it to newspaper ads, Internet ads, bulletin boards, door hangers—whatever your advertising of choice.

Consistency for Procrastinators

The reasons for consistency make a long list. If you place an ad in the newspaper one week, and then don't place an ad for the following twelve weeks, and then place it again for one week . . . do you see the pattern? You may think that advertising once in a while is good enough, but I urge you to think again. Placing an ad only once in a while may produce some business for you, but being consistent will surely be a better bet. People need to see something over and over again before they are "sold" on it—before it sinks into their head deep enough that they need—or at least want—this service badly enough to call and make the appointment.

Think about opening the paper and seeing an ad for a massage therapist. The ad looks so inviting, so you think about it. But then your head tells you to forget it, it's a luxury you can do without right now. Then the following week you see the same ad again, and then again the next week. Sooner or later you will break down and go get the massage. The same is true for people who want to have a personal trainer. One ad may not be enough to convince them, but if they see your ad again and again, it will eventually draw them in and they will succumb to their desire to call you.

Consistency Reduces "Fly-by-Night" Risk

If a potential client is trying to decide between you and another personal trainer, both of whom a friend has recommended, your advertising can make the decision for them. If he or she has heard and seen your name around town in newspapers and other places, this will stick out in his or her mind and likely say to him or her that you are reputable and not going anywhere.

A concern for some potential clients may be that their personal trainer will be a "fly-by-night," meaning the clients prepay for a package and then the trainer disappears with their money. You may shake your head at this, but it is a real concern—don't kid yourself into thinking it isn't. Unfortunately there is a lot of dishonesty in this world. You can help make it a more honest place.

Old Clients = New Clients

Once you are established, whether it takes six months, a year, or longer, you will have a base of new clients right at your fingertips. You will notice some or most of your clients train for a month or two, maybe some train for a long (or permanent) period of time. For sure you will have clients who use your services for a short period

When we were deciding to open a gym on Maui, we had to make the major decision of whether to open a gym with a generic name (Jack Jones' Gym) or invest in a franchise. After careful thought and consideration, the franchise won out. Yes, it was a pricey decision; franchises are not cheap. But when it came to branding and creating a sense of trust from the community, it was worth it. We decided on Powerhouse Gym, and it was a good decision. They helped along the way with opening the gym, and they had an annual convention in Las Vegas, which provided helpful information. (You can go to similar seminars. For more information, see chapter 13).

Buying into the franchise proved to be worthwhile when we were trying to hold presales. Presales are what new gyms do to get members to join their gym prior to opening their doors (usually for a discounted rate to draw them in). This way, once the doors open for business, you have an existing monthly income from all the clients you have already signed up. The overhead of a large fitness facility is too high to operate without an existing membership base from day one.

During this presales period there was hesitation from potential members. Their concern or fear was that it was a hoax, that the gym would not actually open and we would have their credit card information on file. Having the name Powerhouse Gym calmed most everyone's fears and gave us the initial membership base we needed for a successful opening.

As a personal trainer working from your home, you will not have presales, but you will have to create a sense of trust and prove that you have a good reputation. People do not like to hand over their hard-earned money to poeple they do not trust. By consistently advertising, you can earn this trust and create your brand, making you a household name in no time.

of time. By keeping a database of all of your clients, you create your own base of potential clients.

Create a call log and then every six months or so call on that list of clients you formerly trained. Ask them how they are, ask about their family, but keep it short. Then ask them if they would like to train again. Even if they were not thinking about training, the call from you may entice them. Perhaps they like hearing your voice—maybe it triggers feelings of well-being, maybe they have digressed in their health and fitness since last training with you, or perhaps you strike a cord of guilt within them. Whatever the reason, you will end up drumming up some repeat business just by making a few phone calls every so often.

Don't get discouraged if it doesn't work all the time, because surely it won't. You may make calls every six months for two years, twenty maybe thirty calls at a clip, with no positive response. Be persistent, don't give up. This tactic is bound to work sooner or later, and the cost is so minimal, if it even costs anything at all (think free air minutes or unlimited local or long-distance calling plans). It will not be very time-consuming at all; it might take a couple of hours, a couple of times a year. Determination is the key to your success; be persistent.

Creating Your Web Site

Creating a Web site may sound like a scary prospect, but don't look at the big picture—take it one step at a time. It really is not that difficult, and if you need assistance, you can get it.

Domain Name

First you need to get and register your own domain name. It is very important that your business domain name be short and not complicated. I have seen so many people with URLs such as Tammyshomebakeshopdirecttoyou.com. This is way too long and includes too much information! Just as bad is THBS Direct2U.com. Something simple like Tammysbakery.com would be preferable, but because so many domains are already taken, people get carried away and come up with complicated names. It will take some perseverance and creativity to find the right domain name for your business.

A recommended place to search and register available domain names is www.GoDaddy.com. They also have affordable Web site hosting. You can search, buy, and build your Web site all on this server.

E-mail Address

Professionals should never use free e-mail addresses. Using Yahoo!, Gmail, AOL, or other Internet e-mail providers is unprofessional. Obtaining your own e-mail address such as getfit@Lauraspersonaltraining.com will give your business a professional look. It is so simple to get a personalized professional e-mail address. E-mail is low-cost through sites such as GoDaddy.com and says so much about your business. A professional e-mail address adds to the branding of your business as well.

Traditional Web Site

If you just want a traditional Web site, you can do it yourself with many new online tools. Google Sites is one. They are at http://sites.google.com/site/sites. Another site, www.networksolutions.com, will allow you to register your domain and build the site with templates and host it in one place. GoDaddy.com is another option for building a Web site. If you work on a Macintosh computer, try iWeb at www.apple.com/ilife/iweb. There are plenty of others out there, but these are the big ones!

Hiring a Professional Web Designer

Whether or not you should hire a professional Web designer is a tough decision, because honestly there are so many bad designers out there. Most have no formal training and will use the same tools you can use yourself for free. Look for Web sites you like, find out who created them, and compare pricing. A lot of people with a computer think they are Web designers but do very poor work, and they overcharge to boot. Pricing for design will vary from area to area, but you need to make sure you are not getting soaked by an amateur. If the designer does not have a place of business, a professional business card, a clean site of their own, or references, do not pay them a lot of money . . . or better yet, keep shopping.

A professional Web designer will know how to get you into the popular search engines so people can find you. This is very important. A Web site is virtually useless if a search can't drive traffic to the site. It is well worth the money to pay a good, real professional to design and list your site. You might save money by having your nephew design your site, but if no one ever finds your site, you lose money in the long run.

Online Marketing

In today's world, marketing your business online is just about a must-do. Most people look for everything online. The Internet has replaced most other methods of research and how people locate a product or service. You can find opportunities for free marketing online if you get creative, as well as marketing that you would pay for.

Free Online Marketing

What in the world is free these days? Not much! But you can still get free marketing/exposure online. One way is through message boards. You may have been on a message board at some point. There seems to be a message board for everything—planning a trip, learning how to cook, spreading celebrity gossip, looking for the latest fashion . . . you name it, there's a message board for it. So, there are of course fitness message boards as well, and you should use them (when you find the time in your busy day)!

If you live in a high tourism area, go on the travel message boards. An example is Fodors.com, which has sections for each destination. You can target your area and post threads or answer threads for travelers looking for personal trainers in your area. I have seen this work firsthand!

Using the Internet to Get Ahead

As I mentioned, and as I am sure you must know, the Internet is used for just about everything. When someone wants or needs something, they often look to the Internet. There are many ways for you to use the Internet to get ahead in your business. I will mention a few ideas, and you can decide which, if any, you would like to use.

Create a Blog

A blog is basically a Web site where you write your thoughts or make announcements on a daily or other regular basis. The new information you add goes on top, and your readers have the option of commenting or e-mailing you. Blogging started in 1999 and since has reshaped the Web, affected journalism, and enabled millions of people to speak their mind and share their thoughts. You should get in on this action!

The way Internet usage is changing, it is more important than ever to have a social media presence: Facebook, Twitter, and/or a blog. You can even do without a

traditional Web site if you have a blog, and there are several tools that allow anyone
to instantly set up a blog. You can even link your domain to your blog.

Your blog can be like a daily diary or an ongoing story. You can use it to update
your progress with your business. You can tell success stories regarding your clients'
progress in training. You can use your blog to let people know your thoughts about
fitness goals and how to go about achieving them.

Your blog should draw business or at least create a buzz for your business. If
anything, it is a good outlet for yourself and a good way to get feedback, which in
turn can help your business grow.

Craig's List

Craig's List is becoming increasingly popular. It is not just for selling your unwanted
material items; you can also use it to advertise your service, as well as find people
who are looking for your service.

Listing your service on Craig's List is simple and free. The site charges fees only
for job listings and adult and therapeutic services. Craig's List allows you to target
your local area, which in your case is a great advantage. You can post your ad and
then in a week or so, as it moves pages down the list, you can simply log into your
account and delete the old ad and list a new one. It takes all of five minutes. It would
be a smart move to utilize Craig's List.

Facebook

Facebook allows you to connect with real people. And you can attach social actions
and create demand with relevant ads. Advertising on Facebook is not free, however.
Depending on your ad and budget, the minimum cost is $1 per day. Not bad for a
month! And you can even include photos.

To create an ad, Facebook walks you through a step-by-step process. Once you get set up, a nice feature is that you can track your ad to see how many "clicks" it gets. The cost of your ad may fluctuate depending on the amount of "clicks" you get. So, keep an eye on what you are spending and make sure you are not throwing your money away. If your traffic is not what you want it to be, you can modify your ad until it works to your satisfaction.

Another nice thing about Facebook is that you can create a social buzz about your services right on your "wall." With the help of your friends—and your wall—you can build your business for free. If you are a Facebook user (or FB junkie, as I like to call myself), you know what I am talking about. If not, I urge you to take a look at Facebook.com. The networking site makes it very easy to connect with friends and then with friends of friends within your own community. With the correct settings, whatever you post on your wall is viewable by every connection you have, right on their home page. This is a great way to market a local business such as your home-based personal trainer business! You can post exercise and health clips off of You-Tube, plus fitness-related articles or any information you want.

More Sites to Get Noticed

There are so many choices these days as far as social networking and connecting with friends, old friends, and new friends. I mentioned Facebook already, but there are many more options. MySpace (www.myspace.com) is another major social network site. Both Facebook and MySpace are great for letting people know what you do and what you specialize in and just making contacts, whether friendships or business

The Need for Caution

Although the Internet is a powerful marketing tool, there is a need for caution—a valid need. Be very careful about who you attract online. I don't mean to scare you, but this is serious. Think before you decide whom you will let into your home. When you advertise online, you open yourself up to a whole realm of people.

You might want to wait to see if you will even need to advertise online. A Web site is something you should have for sure. And when you advertise on your Facebook page, you limit your exposure to just your "friend" list.

relationships. Friends can be clients, too. Quite often, especially in the personal training business, you will end up with friends as clients. Facebook and MySpace are great venues to grow your friend clientele, and as important, gain friends of friends as clients (or at least contacts, which may eventually lead to clients).

There are several other Web sites that you can use for the same purpose that put a little less information all over the site.

LinkedIn (www.LinkedIn.com) is a professional site for business contacts. You can be introduced to professionals in your field and use it as a networking system.

Classmates (www.Classmates.com) is a good site to get reacquainted with old friends from school. This is especially a good idea if you still live in the town/city you grew up in. It is much less relevant if you grew up in New York and now live in San Francisco. But any kind of networking helps.

Twitter (www.Twitter.com) is the newest of these sites and has become very popular very quickly! I am sure you have heard of "tweeting," and chances are you already use Twitter (or any of the above sites). Twitter is a site that allows you to communicate in shorter text-like posts.

Grow and Maintain

The networking sites mentioned above are great for creating contacts and new business, but they also offer a wonderful communication highway that you can use between you and your clients. This kind of communication can help you maintain your relationship with your existing clients. Constant contact and communication will lend a hand in keeping your clients training with you. The more contact you have with your clients while they are actively training with you, the stronger the bond you will build, leading to a longer relationship, which means a longer-term client for you. The ultimate benefit for you is a more successful business.

12

Business Endgame: Stay Small, Grow, or Sell

Reaching Success

What makes you a success? Is it when you start making enough money to live comfortably? Is it when your reputation is glowing and clients are contacting you without you having to look for them? It is up to each business owner to decide when he or she has become successful. You will know when this time arrives for you. A feeling of satisfaction will overcome you.

Once that happens, however, you will be faced with other questions—and possibly fears. These may include: What if the economy takes a downturn? What if a few of my steady clients decide to stop training at the same time? Either of these could happen at any given time. So, always be prepared, and never get too confident that your success is here to stay. You should always, no matter how "successful" you are, keep working at improving and maintaining your business.

Are You Satisfied?

People who own their own successful business deal with the success in different ways. When you feel you have built your business to capacity, that there is no room for any more clients and you are making enough money and then some, you may feel satisfied with what you have accomplished. But what do you do about that feeling of satisfaction?

When you feel satisfied, are you the type of person who is okay with being satisfied, or do you want more? Every person is different. Some people want to glide along for the ride as long as they are satisfied, while others are never fully satisfied. Once they get a taste of success, they want more, more, and more.

No matter which personality you are, do what is best for yourself and what will make you happiest. In this chapter I will discuss different options and scenarios that you may entertain once you have reached success or feel satisfied.

Bringing in Additional Trainers

You may consider bringing in additional trainers who will want to work out of your studio. Here are two reasons why you may want to consider this option:

- You have reached your capacity of hours; you have so many clients that you cannot fit any more into your schedule.
- You would like to bring in additional income without actually doing the work.

If you have reached the limit of hours you can work and would like to still make more money, having trainers work out of your studio is a viable option. Before you do this, however, ask yourself the following questions:

- Can two trainers work out of my studio at the same time (is it large enough)?
- If not, are there enough hours in the day open for other trainers to use my studio?
- Am I prepared to handle the issues that may come along with having trainers other than myself work out of my home/studio?

If you decide that bringing in additional trainers is something you would like to explore, consider the following two options.

Employees

Hiring employees brings all kinds of red tape. You will need to pay them and take out taxes (which you can do through financial software, such as QuickBooks). You will also be responsible for their liability insurance coverage. This can become a hassle and maybe even expensive for you, not to mention time-consuming.

Most often, trainers will not want to be considered "employees" anyway, but it is an option. The more popular way to go about having a trainer work out of your studio is to have them be an "independent contractor."

Independent Contractors

Having someone work for you as an independent contractor is a good way to go. An independent contractor gets his or her own insurance, and you should not permit the trainer to work out of your studio until you have a copy of proof of that insurance. If a trainer is working in your studio and his or her client gets hurt, it is imperative that the trainer has insurance, or your entire business can go down the tubes!

An independent contractor will also be the one paying *you*. Sounds good to me! There are two ways the trainer(s) can pay you. One option is that he or she pays a base rent. The other is that he or she gives you a percentage of his or her clients' fees.

Rent

Rent usually works well if the trainer has unlimited access to your facility. With your studio in your home, most likely you do not want the trainer to have unlimited access; rather, you want him or her to schedule sessions around your sessions. Having a separate entrance for your studio, however, would be a good bonus when it comes to having additional trainers.

The amount of rent to charge is influenced by several factors: Geography is one. If you live in New York City, you can charge a higher rent versus living in Charleston, South Carolina. You also want to factor in how often the trainer plans to utilize your studio. You can start at one rate and then go on a sliding scale. This way, if the trainer starts out using your studio only a couple of hours a week, and then jumps to twenty or so hours per week, you are also able to reap the rewards.

Percentage of Client Fee

Having the trainer(s) pay you a percentage is a popular way to go about bringing in other trainers. The percentage varies; usually it is a 60/40, 70/30, or 80/20 split. The trainer gets the higher percentage.

A flat fee is what I have usually done with my independent trainers. I like it because then I don't have to worry if the trainers are being honest about how much they are charging their clients and if the amount they are paying me is correct. The fee per session can range from $15 per session to $25 per session. You should do some research in your local area to see what the going rate is.

Becoming an Employer—You Are the Boss

When you decide to have trainers work out of your studio, whether they are employees or independent contractors, you are the boss. It is your studio, therefore your rules. It is imperative that you take on this role from the beginning. Personal trainers can have very big egos (from my observations), and they may try to set their own rules in your studio. If you let them know from the very beginning that you are the boss, you should not have any problems with this. Once you slip and let the trainers walk all over you, it will be that much more difficult to put yourself in the management role and to gain back their respect.

There are several ways that trainers may try to step on your toes. For example, they may come in to use your studio at unscheduled times, or perhaps they do not pay you on time. Maybe they do not clean up your studio after their sessions. All of these, plus other situations, are ones for which you should have a zero-tolerance policy. If the trainers know you are serious from the beginning, chances are they will not try to cross you. This does not mean you have to be rude, just firm. There is a difference. You can have policies and gain respect and still be a likeable person. There is a fine line, and it does take practice, but it is doable.

During the interview process, have potential candidates fill out an application, such as the one below. When bringing in an independent contractor, have them sign a Personal Training Agreement, below as well. It's necessary to have everything you agree upon with an independent contractor in writing.

Probation Period

With most jobs there is a probation period for new employees. Whether you have brought in a trainer as an employee or as an independent contractor, I suggest you implement a six-month probation period. (For jobs that are consistent, everyday jobs, three months may be all that's needed. But the trainer(s) you hire will most likely not be working every day, especially in the beginning.)

The purpose of a probation period is to give you time to see if a trainer will be a good fit and an asset to your business. Having a probation period relieves you of the stress of bringing someone in and having to worry about him or her not working up to your standards. It should be clear to the trainer that you can terminate him or her at any given time with no recourse. This does not mean that you should ask him or her to leave after one slipup. You should instead give the trainer every chance to prove him- or herself worthy of being a part of your business.

Your Reputation Comes First

One very important aspect to keep in mind when bringing in trainers is that they represent you and your business. They will be linked to your business in the minds of the community, their clients, and your clients. If they conduct themselves in a manner that is contradictory to your own behavior, or if their level of professionalism is

EMPLOYMENT APPLICATION

Name:_____ Date:_____

Address:_____

City:_____ State:_____ Zip:_____

Phone:(_____)_____ Social Security #:_____

Fax or Cell:(_____)_____ Email:_____

Are you over the age of 21? ☐ Yes ☐ No Birth Date:_____

Job for which applying:_____

Do you have experience? ☐ Yes ☐ No Any professional designations:_____

Are there any days/hours that you are not available to work?_____
_____

EMPLOYMENT HISTORY:

Company:_____ From:_____ To:_____

Address:_____City:_____ State:_____ Zip:_____

Phone:(_____)_____ Fax:(_____)_____

Job Duties:_____
_____

Reason for Leaving:_____
_____

Name of Supervisor:_____ Salary:$_____ p/hour or $_____ p/month

Company:_____ From:_____ To:_____

Address:_____City:_____ State:_____ Zip:_____

Phone:(_____)_____ Fax:(_____)_____

Job Duties:_____
_____

Reason for Leaving:_____
_____

Name of Supervisor:_____ Salary:$_____ p/hour or $_____ p/month

Do you have any medical problems that we should be aware of? e.g. (back problems, heart, breathing, etc): ☐ Yes ☐ No   If Yes, Explain:_____
_____

Have you ever been convicted of a Felony? ☐ Yes ☐ No   If Yes, Explain:_____
_____

Person to Notify in Case of Emergency:

Name:_____ Phone:(_____)_____

Address:_____City:_____State:_____

Relationship:_____ Note:_____

Signature:_____ Date:_____

For Office Use:
Hire:_____Start Date:_____Start Salary:$_____per_____

Laura's Studio Personal Training Agreement

Name: _____ Signature: _____ Date: _____

             Trainer   Trainer

Start-Up Requirements
    1. Personal training certification
    2. Minimum $1,000,000.00 liability insurance - Provide current copy of coverage
    3. Current CPR/First Aid Certification Card

A copy of your Personal Training Certificate and proper insurance coverage, minimum $1,000,000, must be on hand before training.

Split Fees with Studio
☐ Level 4 = 40% Club – 60% Trainer
    1. All new trainers start at Level 1 for a 90 day period
    2. Certification with ACE (American Council on Exercise), IFPA (International Fitness Professionals Association), NFPT (National Federation of Professional Trainers), ISSA (International Sports Sciences Association)

☐ Level 3 = 35% Club – 65% Trainer
    1. Certification with ACSM or NSCA
    2. Well-written business plan

☐ Level 2 = 30% Club – 70% Trainer
    1. Associates degree as a fitness specialist
    2. Certification with either ACSM or NSCA
    3. Well-written business plan

☐ Level 1 = 25% Club – 75% Trainer
    1. Bachelor's in Exercise Science or Exercise Physiology
    2. Certification with ACSM (American College of Sports Medicine) and NSCA (National Strength & Conditioning Association)
    3. Exceptional business plan

Code of Conduct
As an Independent Trainer, you represent yourself and Laura's Studio. You are responsible for conducting yourself professionally at all times. This includes adhering to all rules and guidelines set forth by Laura's Studio, which may change from time to time. Example: Excessive tardiness of clients is not professional and may be cause for termination of your training privileges.

All clients are obligated to fill out a Trainer/Client Agreement that waives all misconduct, responsibility, negligence, and such from Laura's Studio. This form will be signed and turned in to Laura's Studio management before training begins with each client. If a Trainer/Client Agreement is not signed, clients may not be trained on the premises of Laura's Studio until agreement is signed.

Support and **Respect** of each trainer is not a consideration, it is a requirement. If it comes to the attention of any trainer or management that a fellow trainer is acting in an unprofessional manner, it will be up to the entire training staff and management as to the future of this particular trainer. At any time, fellow trainers may vote, majority ruling, to decide if the unprofessional trainer may continue business in the club. This rule is to prohibit conflict amongst trainers and promote team morale and professional team ethics.

Dress Code
New, clean tennis shoes—no open-toed shoes, as required by our insurance carrier. Laura's Studio T-shirt. Your cost will be our cost + tax. Consult the Head Personal Trainer about purchasing your size & quantity of shirts. Clothing must be washed and pressed. No jean material.

I have read and understand the above. I will begin rent on: _____

Signature: _____ Date: _____ Witness: _____
                  Trainer   Laura's Studio Rep.
Contact Phone #: _____

not where it needs to be, this could potentially harm your reputation and ultimately your business.

If a trainer has potential—and I am sure you would not hire a person if you did not see potential there to begin with—counsel him or her after you notice less-than-stellar behavior. Often employees do not realize their own actions can affect the business. So a simple meeting where you address the issue may be all that is needed to remedy the situation. An open line of communication between you and anyone you bring into your establishment is key to the success of your expansion.

Noncompete Agreement

As in many businesses, employees or independent contractors may use your business as a stepping stone to build their future business venture. You can and should protect yourself from trainers who use your business to grow their own clientele and then branch out and open their own studio, ultimately resulting in taking clients away from your business, hurting your business, and becoming competition.

A noncompete agreement can help you avoid this problem. This agreement can state that a trainer whom you hire cannot open a personal training business within a certain number of miles of your business and cannot go to work for a competitor. Both clauses would include a certain length of time.

An attorney can draw up a noncompete agreement for you, and then both you and the trainer need to sign it. It is a pretty standard agreement, so don't worry that it would be too costly. After all, protecting yourself and your business is a wise investment.

Setting Quotas

What your business does not need is "dead weight." The reason you would hire a trainer would be to expand your business, with the bottom line being to make more money. Especially if you hire trainers as employees, you will want to set goals for them that they must reach in order to remain a trainer for you. Start off with easily attainable goals. You don't want to make it too difficult, which could potentially set up your employees for failure. Give them a fair chance to prove themselves. An attainable goal gives them the opportunity to grow their client base, in turn growing your business. Raise the goal, within reason, each month, or more realistically, every three or even six months, until the goal is high enough to be well worth it for you and the trainer.

Once the trainers have proven themselves as reputable trainers who are an asset to your business and increase your revenue, come up with incentives for them. Normally an incentive would be a monetary bonus or a gift of some nature. Money would be the incentive to drive them to do their best for you—it always is!

If your trainers are valuable to you, it is your duty to keep them happy. Never take a good employee for granted. Make sure they know they are appreciated. Say thank you to them, buy them lunch, give them a bonus—do something, anything, to let them know you appreciate and value them. If you have ever worked for someone (which I am sure at one point or another you have), you know that a little appreciation goes a long way. No one wants to feel like he or she does not matter or is not serving a purpose. Making your employees feel appreciated is very important to keeping them with you.

If you have trainers who are independent contractors, you might still want to set minimum monthly goals, or you can opt for the monthly rent. This ensures that you do not have a lazy trainer with your business name attached to them.

Selling Products

When you first open, you want to concentrate on your main focus, which is building your clientele. Once you have established yourself and have a nice base of clients whom you feel comfortable with, you want to look for other ways to grow your business.

Selling products can be a great way to increase revenue. Granted, you will not have a large group of people coming through your doors in your home studio, but you can still make a profit if you are savvy.

Marketing your products is key. If you have products to sell, put them on a shelf, and never do anything else, they will do nothing for you except give you something to use your feather duster on. Introduce your products to your clients and sell them on your Web site. Talk to people; let them know you are selling products.

What will you sell? You can sell products such as exercise apparel, weight-lifting gloves, belts, and wrist wraps. You can also sell supplements or anything else you can come up with that has to do with fitness. Go ahead and be creative!

Your Brand/Logo

In chapter 5 I talked about "branding your business." You can use your logo, which is an important element of your brand, when you decide what products you should sell. If you get exercise tops made with your logo on them, you are making a double bonus for yourself. Not only are you making a profit on the merchandise you sell, you are also creating "walking billboards." Every time one of your clients (or customers) wears something that has your logo on it, he or she is advertising for you.

Here are some items you can sell with your brand/logo:

- T-shirts
- Men's tank tops
- Ladies' sports bras
- Exercise shorts
- Socks
- Water bottles

Supplements

If you are going to sell supplements, shop around with different vendors. There are so many choices when it comes to supplements. A good way to choose is to go with

Hit the Streets

You want your name (brand/logo) to be known in your community. This is the ultimate recognition—to be a household name.

An idea to help make this happen is to invest some cash in inexpensive items that you can give to your clients, friends, family, and so on. Think of the expense as advertising/marketing costs (which is what you will categorize the purchase under in your financial software). Here are some ideas:

- Pens
- Key chains
- Sticky note pads
- Water bottles
- Stress balls (the kind you squeeze in your hand)
- Magnets
- Koozies (the sleeve you put on beer/soda cans to keep them cold)

a brand you know and have used. It is much easier to sell a product that you have firsthand experience with and believe in.

Some vendors you might want to look into are Champion Nutrition (championnutrition.com), Nutri-Force Nutrition (Nutriforce.com), WholesaleSupplementStore.com, or A1supplements.com. These are just a few choices; there are hundreds out there. Research online or go into local stores such as Vitamin World or GNC to find out what sells best.

Adding Elements

There are so many options when it comes to expanding your business. Adding new elements to your business is a great way to broaden your spectrum of possibilities.

Boot Camp

Boot camp has become immensely popular. There are indoor boot camp classes in fitness centers and—my favorite—outdoor boot camps held in parks or on the beach.

Starting a boot camp class can really pick up your momentum. You can advertise in the local paper and get your clients involved. Have them recruit their friends and/or family to come take your class. You can either charge each person per class, or establish boot camp classes that last four weeks (or whatever length you choose) and meet maybe two or three times per week. This way, each participant pays a flat fee for the entire four-week class, whether they show up or not. This will make it easier for you to balance your budget (instead of not knowing how many people will be paying for each class). This also gets people to make a commitment and increases the chance that they will take your next boot camp class as well!

If you opt to do an outdoor activity, have your participants sign a separate waiver for this event. Here is an example:

Laura's Boot Camp
Special Event Waiver and Release Form

You, the participant, are aware that you are engaging in physical exercise and/or a special event that may cause serious injury or even death to you. You are hereby advised that you should be sufficiently physically fit to participate in these activities and should have consulted a physician prior to undertaking this or any physical exercise program.

If you are injured while participating in this or any program sponsored by Laura's Boot Camp, you agree to "hold harmless" Laura's Boot Camp, including any officers or employees. You hereby waive all rights that you might otherwise have to sue. You understand that this waiver applies regardless of negligence or fault.

Name of participant: _____

Signature: _____

Date: ____/____/____

Group Classes

Depending on the amount of space you have, you may want to entertain the idea of group fitness classes. Even if you have room for just four or five people, group classes can be a great way to build momentum and introduce potential clients to you and your services.

There is a wide range of choices when it comes to group fitness: You can offer yoga, Pilates, kickboxing, and/or fit ball. You can even spice it up with dance classes such as salsa or hip-hop. Another class that has become popular these days is pole dancing (but that's a whole other book . . .).

For a fee structure, you can charge per class or offer packages, such as ten classes for a slightly discounted rate.

House Calls

I have run into this a few times—people who prefer to work out in their own home. This may be an idea that you will want to consider. Not to stereotype, but most often it is the wealthiest people who like the trainer to come to their house. Maybe it is the comfort of their own home that they like. Whatever the reason, if this is what they want, bring the gym to them!

Making house calls will require you to think outside the box and maybe come out of *your* comfort zone. You obviously will not be carrying your functional trainer with you to the clients' homes, but you can bring some tools to make this happen. Easy-to-transport items include fit balls, resistance bands, and so on. Perhaps the client has a home gym and you could use some of his or her own equipment, too.

Covering More Fields

Are you ready to branch out? If you are like me, you always want to strive for more, continue to learn, and achieve as much as you can. (By achieve, I don't mean monetarily, although that is nice also. I mean continue to grow and challenge your mind.)

If you are itching to grow in this way, becoming knowledgeable and possibly certified in other fields, such as nutrition, is a good way to expand your business and your mind. After all, being able to offer your clients more than personal training can work to your advantage monetarily and help you keep your clients attached to

> **Take Note**
>
> All of these add-on elements are of course optional. I want to give you ideas on ways you can expand your business. Use some of them, all of them, or none of them—but just know what your options are. In addition to earning additional income from these options, you should also be able to gain new personal training clients from them.

you. If you offer them more services, this will improve the chances of them feeling connected to you and possibly like they need you.

For example, if you were to become a certified nutritionist, you would open up a whole other realm of personal service to your clients. You would be able to offer them a complete package. You would train their body as well as their eating habits. Such a combination would make you that much more efficient and dynamic.

Teaching Trainers

One more way to expand your business is by teaching new trainers, or people who want to become trainers. Everyone learns from someone, so why not become that teacher? Up-and-coming trainers can get certified online or in a classroom. You can offer one-on-one training for people who like the hands-on—in front of you—learning technique.

Do You Have Selling on Your Mind?

Chances are you are thinking: "What? I haven't even started my business yet!" Okay, so I am just covering all the bases here. There may come a time when you feel it is time to move on or to try new ventures. There may be several reasons why you would contemplate selling your business.

Selling would include the sale of your equipment, tools, and clients. All of your clients may not go with the new owner, but that would be their decision.

An Offer You Can't Refuse

Once your business is established, there is a chance that a fellow trainer may want to buy your business. If someone makes you an offer that sounds good, crunch the numbers, maybe run it by your accountant. If it turns out to be an "offer you can't refuse," then you may just want to take it.

A New Dream

Not to get into different fields here . . . but it can happen. You may decide that you want to pursue different avenues or different professions. Things come up in life that you don't expect, sometimes causing you to want to make a change, or maybe an intriguing opportunity presents itself to you.

Life is funny like that. You just never know what will fall in your lap, or what turn of events will happen to cause you to make a huge change. When life calls, sometimes you can't pass it up. If you have a new dream or new passion, go for it. After all, you didn't become a successful personal trainer without passion.

Should an opportunity arise for a different career, selling your business would then become something to think about. In taking on a new venture, selling could be the best thing for you. Here is where some personal trainers make a big mistake; they don't sell, but rather end their training and leave their clients to find new trainers. This leaves you with nothing to show for all of your hard work and efforts, and it will result in you leaving your clients in a lurch. By selling your business to a worthy buyer, you are being compensated for the business you built and your clients will be able to continue training with little or no interruption. You'll be showing your professionalism to the very end.

Obstacles to Selling

There will be obstacles to selling your business. As you have probably figured out by now, nothing is that easy. When it comes to your business, most everything takes effort, perseverance, and a bit of strategic planning.

One obstacle may be if your clients find out too early that you are thinking of selling your business. This may cause them to move on to a new trainer before you are ready for them to do so. Keep the idea of selling as private as you can. If you use a business broker, there should be a confidentiality agreement.

A further obstacle can be deciding what price to put on your business. You have worked so hard to make your business a success, so before selling, come up with a target selling price. As I mentioned earlier, if you are not sure, speak with your accountant. If someone makes you an offer without you ever having to put your business on the market, that saves you a lot of effort. That would be the "offer you can't refuse."

Once you come up with a price, the next obstacle is how to sell your business. You can try to sell your business on your own by placing ads in the newspaper and online. Do not expect it to be easy though. You may want to consider hiring a business broker. Yes, you will have to pay a fee, but sometimes it is worth it when someone else handles most of the legwork and headaches for you.

If you are ready to sell, you have made it to this point. You should consider yourself lucky! The fact that you have started a business and built it up to the point of being able to sell it for a profit is a huge accomplishment. Be proud of yourself!

13

Training and Certification

Certified Personal Trainer

One of the very first things you need to do before opening your business (if you have not already) is become a certified personal trainer. There are so many options for certifications. There are different schools, online courses, and so on. Plus you can continue your education even after you are certified. Continuing your education, therefore increasing your knowledge and expertise, is always a good idea.

Focus on Your Strengths

When deciding on certifications, look at your strengths and interests. You will be that much more valuable to your clients if you focus on something that you are adept at and passionate about. If you have always been an avid weight trainer, chances are your passion will exude while training others. If you have always been a fan of yoga, then perhaps you will want to incorporate yoga into your training. Now, of course your training will depend on each individual client, but if you use your strengths in your regimen, it is very likely your clients will see the professionalism and skill you ultimately want to portray.

You will need to get an overall personal training certification for sure. But what I am saying here is that you can get additional certifications in specialized areas. This will look very impressive to your clients.

Go Outside Your Comfort Zone

I just suggested that you focus on your strengths and areas of interest, and that is a good idea—one that may benefit you and your clients in the long run. However, to be considered one of the best personal trainers in your area and to become very successful, you will sometimes have to go outside of your comfort zone. Maybe you are interested in all areas of personal training, but this is unlikely.

Maybe you are keen on plyometrics but not too into training for bodybuilding. Or perhaps you are an expert on yoga but not very knowledgeable about weight training. No matter what your areas of comfort and knowledge, to be the "full package" that your clients will be looking for, you should acquire training in all areas of personal training. The general certification for personal training covers an overall blanket of training. In addition to becoming a certified personal trainer, I suggest you study individual areas with the intention of becoming as knowledgeable and efficient at training as you can.

Don't Forget the Less Obvious

Okay, so you know you will get certified as a personal trainer (if you are not already), and maybe (hopefully) you will study up on some specific areas to gain additional knowledge. With that in mind, here is more to think about! These are training courses in areas you may not have thought about:

- **Fitness testing.** Learn the most important, popular, and essential exercise tests you can use to perform fitness assessment, exercise prescription, and program design.
- **Safety guidelines.** This is a course on how to train your clients and keep them injury free.
- **Program design specialist.** You can learn to design training programs for each of your clients. Keep your clients from reaching plateaus and help them reach ultimate results. *This is a certification course.*

If you are interested in these or other courses, here are sites that offer them:

- **IFPA (International Fitness Professionals Association) Personal Trainer Certification (www.ifpa-fitness.com/index.php)** Offers certification and training courses in all of the areas above, plus many more! I highly recommend taking a look at this site. It offers comprehensive information on many courses, as well as certifications and how to go about studying.
- **National Academy of Sports Medicine (NASM)** (www.nasm.org)
- **American Council on Exercise (ACE)** (www.acefitness.org)

NCCA versus Non-NCCA

In your case, starting your own personal trainer business, NCCA-accredited personal training courses are your best choice. NCCA stands for the National Commission for Certifying Agencies. The NCCA accredits programs that meet its standards. While there are several other organizations that attempt to offer accreditation, the NCCA is the one that seems to matter most. The major exceptions to this rule, however, are personal training degrees and certifications offered by reputable colleges and trade schools. Most of these programs are accredited by the government and do not bother to go through the NCCA.

There are several very good non-NCCA programs out there, but they will not give your reputation the boost it needs. You may decide to take some non-NCCA courses just to improve your knowledge. These courses are usually less expensive and easier to complete.

The American Council on Exercise (ACE) and the National Academy of Sports Medicine (NASM) are two very popular and credible certification programs (NCCA accredited) and cost $400 to $800 for certification.

Classroom Programs

While classroom programs, or workshops, can be expensive, especially if you have to travel to another city, they are your best option for training and certification. The most reputable certifications all have workshop programs to get you certified. You will acquire hands-on experience and leave with the most abundant knowledge possible.

The most reputable certification courses (workshops) are approximately two days long and held in most major U.S. cities. If you live in a major city and do not have to travel to take one of these workshops, don't even think twice about it—this is the way to go. If you live in a remote town or city and will have to travel, you could be looking at a big expense by the time you factor in airfare and hotel costs on top of the cost of the actual course. However, if you can manage to do this, it would be a wise investment.

Online Programs

Online certification programs are becoming increasingly popular, which only makes sense these days. If you live in an area where you can easily take a workshop program, I again highly recommend that you take it. If you do not live in an area that offers workshops, and you are unable to travel for one reason or another, then you can opt for an online program. Two very reputable online programs are Pinnacle (www.pinnaclepersonaltraining.com) and Penn Foster (www.pennfoster.edu).

Keeping Current with Recertifications

Most personal training certifications require a renewal every two to three years. It is very important that you become recertified when the time comes. Keeping current with your certification is important to your status and credibility. In addition to keeping your certification current because you are "supposed to," you should also want to continue to learn and keep the knowledge fresh in your mind. What's more, it can help ensure the safety of your clients. Striving to be the best takes hard work and perseverance, so roll up your sleeves and get to work.

Fitness and Personal Training Seminars

Pretend for a minute that you work for a large corporation. The company will most likely hold conventions, conferences, training seminars, and so on. Why? To keep its employees at the top of their game.

Attending fitness seminars is something you should do. It is not always easy, depending on where you live, but if it is feasible, periodically check to see where the nearest reputable seminar will be and try to attend it (or as many as you can). It can only help you!

Fitness Expos

Aside from being very informative, fitness expos can also be a lot of fun. Expos include so many variables, from taking seminars that help increase your knowledge and confidence, to meeting top vendors of products and equipment. You can learn about all of the latest trends in fitness, as well as network with hundreds or thousands of folks all in your field. Expos are held around the country at various times throughout the year, usually in major cities such as New York, Los Angeles, and Las Vegas.

CPR Certification

CPR certification is a requirement of being a certified personal trainer. For most certified personal trainer (CPT) courses, it is a prerequisite to be CPR certified.

CPR Savers Training

The American Association of CPR Life Savers & First Aid Safety is a comprehensive program that offers a wide range of safety training classes in automated external defibrillators (AEDs), CPR, and first aid. It also has all the necessary training supplies you might need. CPR classes are currently being held in groups of a maximum of ten students. The class is approximately three hours long.

For locations and cost call (800) 480-1277, or visit the Web site at www.cpr-savers-training.com/index.html.

American Red Cross

The American Red Cross (ARC) offers training and certification in CPR, first aid, and AED. The ARC offers consistency across the nation with trained professionals, which gives you the confidence that you are receiving top-notch training. Classes can be scheduled at your convenience. They are cost-effective and developed by experts. For more information contact your local ARC or visit their Web site at www.redcross.org.

Certifications Can Improve Your Business

Quality is important when it comes to certification. As mentioned earlier in this chapter, some certifications hold more prestige than others (NCCA vs. Non-NCCA), so you want to make good choices when deciding which certification to achieve. Once you are certified, don't stop there. Continue to learn, grow, and obtain as much knowledge as you can. You should never feel that you know it all. There is always room to grow, more knowledge to obtain, and more expertise to strive for.

When you receive your certificates of certification, frame them and hang them on the wall in your studio—just like doctors do. This will surely impress your clients. They will see that you have an abundance of training, and they will feel confident that you are knowledgeable and that they are in good hands.

In addition to gaining respect and confidence from your clients, more certifications justify a higher price. Because you have acquired more certifications than the average trainer in your town, you can charge on the higher end of the average price of a personal trainer.

First Aid Certification

Obtaining first aid certification is not a requirement, but it is something you should seriously consider—especially because you will be training clients in your home, where it will often be just you and your client, meaning no one else around to help in an emergency.

Your hope is to not have any emergencies or injuries that would require you to have to use your first aid or CPR training. But the reality is that emergencies and injuries do happen: People have heart attacks while running on a treadmill and they cut themselves on equipment—anything can happen, and you want to be prepared!

In a true emergency, you should always call 911 immediately. But it can take ten or twenty minutes for the paramedics to arrive. In the meantime, because you are trained, you can make the situation better or even save a life.

In Conclusion

Congratulations, you have finished the book! My hope is that you found it useful and it gave you the confidence and reassurance you need to go out there and build the best home-based personal trainer business this world has ever seen!

I enjoyed writing this book, and even learned a thing or two myself during the process. My best wishes to you for all the success and happiness in the world!

Certification Resources

Certification School Comparisons
www.starting-a-personal-training-business.com/personal-training-certification-school.html

Personal Training Schools in Your Area
www.naturalhealers.com/feat-personaltraining.shtml?msnad=PT_certified_personal_trainer&src=msnad_anh_cert_pers_trai_210838

National Board of Fitness Examiners
www.nbfe.org/about/affiliate

ISSA Seminars (International Sports Sciences Association) Online Certification
www.issaonline.com/fitness-seminars

ISSA—Youth Fitness Trainer Certification
www.issaonline.com/certification/youth-fitness-trainer.cfm

ISSA—Specialist for Fitness in Older Adults
www.issaonline.com/certification/specialist-in-fitness-for-older-adults.cfm

ISSA—Fitness Therapist Certification (Disabled)
www.issaonline.com/certification/fitness-therapist.cfm

GFFI—Fitness Academy (home study)
Exercise programming for special populations, (i.e., children, seniors, pre-/postnatal, and more.)
www.gffi-fitness.org/PersTrain.htm

Starting a Personal Training Business—Personal Trainer Certification Course—Prep Course
Training special populations (children, seniors, obese, injured persons)
www.starting-a-personal-training-business.com/personal-training-certification-school.html

AFPA—Trainer of Special Populations Certificate
www.afpafitness.com/store/index.php?main_page=index&cPath=1_23

Certification

NASM (The National Academy of Sports Medicine)
www.nasm.org/

NASM Recertification
www.nasm.org/search.aspx?q=recertification

ACE (American Council on Exercise)
www.acefitness.org/

NSCA (National Strength and Conditioning Association)
www.nsca-cc.org/

AFTA (Aerobic Fitness Trainers Association)
www.aftacertification.com/index.html

NCSF (National Council on Strength and Fitness)
www.ncsf.org/pdf/ncsf_certification_course.pdf

CPR and First Aid

CPR Savers & First Aid Supply
www.cpr-savers.com

CPR Savers Training
www.cpr-savers-training.com

American Red Cross
www.redcross.org/

American AED
www.americanaed.com

Equipment

Free Motion Fitness
(877) 363-8449
www.freemotionfitness.com

Precor
(800) 786-8404
www.precor.com

Nordic Track
www.Nordictrack.com

Bowflex
(800) 886-6582
www.bowflex.com

Star Trac Fitness Direct
(800) 745-3815
www.startracusa.com

Life Fitness
(800) 634-8637
www.lifefitness.com

Equipment Accessories

Power Systems
www.power-systems.com

Club Purchasing Service
www.club-supplies.com

Yoga Direct
www.yogadirect.com

Healthy Styles Exercise Equipment
www.healthystylesexercise.com

Kettlebells
Dragon Door
www.dragondoor.com

Warehouse Fitness (equipment and accessories)
www.warehousefitness.com

Total Trainer (adjustable dumbbells)
(800) 230-1256
www.total-trainer.com/Dumbbells

Power Block (dumbbells, adjustable dumbbells)
(800) 446-5215
www.powerblock.com

Bowflex Select Tech Dumbbells
(800) 436-7887
www.bowflexselecttech.com

Body Fat Calipers
www.sport-fitness-advisor.com/bodyfatcalipers.html

Mirrors (shatterproof)
http://thebarrecompany.com

Used/Refurbished Equipment

Global Fitness

(888) 991-9991

www.global-fitness.com/landing

Fitness Rush

www.fitnessrush.com/exercise-equipment-mats.html

Seminars and Expos

Phil Kaplan, "The Fitness Truth"—Seminar

www.philkaplan.com/thefitnesstruth/seminars.htm

Power Systems—Total Training Seminar

http://totaltrainingseminars.com

Fitness Expos

Los Angeles Fitness Expo

www.thefitexpo.com

Health and Wellness Fairs

www.health-and-wellness-fairs.com

Branding and Logos

Branding Your Business

www.entrepreneur.com/marketing/branding/article35446.html

Logo Maker by Hewlitt Packard

www.logomaker.com

Online Marketing

Online Advertising (links)

www.Hubspot.com

Google

www.google.com/local

Blogs

https://www.blogger.com/start

www.Blogspot.com

www.Wordpress.com

Domain and Web Sites

www.GoDaddy.com

http://sites.google.com/sites/sites

www.networksolutions.com

www.apple.com/ilife/iweb

SBA Loans

www.sba.gov/aboutsba/index.html

Zoning Laws

WorkatHome.org

www.work-at-home.org/sreport/home-based-businesses/12.htm

Backup Devices

www.ehow.com/how_2500_choose-backup-storage.html

Medical Dictionary

http://medical-dictionary.thefreedictionary.com

Business Plans

www.bplans.com

www.sba.gov/smallbusinessplanner/plan/writeabusinessplan

www.businessplans.org/index.asp

Office Furniture and Supplies

Simply Desks

www.simplydesks.com

Ergonomic Chairs

www.ergonomicofficechairs.com

Beyond the Office Door
www.beyondtheofficedoor.com

Office Depot
www.officedepot.com

OfficeMax
www.officemax.com

Staples
www.Staples.com

Filing Cabinets
www.filingcabinets.com

Home Decorators
www.homedecorators.com

Mirrors

The Barre Company
http://thebarrecompany.com

GymMirror.com
www.gymmirror.com

Rubber Flooring

Kodiak Sports
www.kodiaksports.com/rubberweightroomflooring.aspx?gclid=CPfFsePOs5sCFQ9J
agodnGkLQQ

Rubber Flooring Inc.
www.rubberflooringinc.com

Great Mats
www.greatmats.com

Index

About the Author

Laura Augenti has been involved in the fitness industry for more than fifteen years. Currently she specializes in weight training, core training including Pilates, and boot camp training. In addition, Laura has organized running clubs and assisted clients training for marathons and races. In 2005 Laura cofounded Powerhouse Gym on Maui, Hawaii, which attracted celebrity clients such as Arnold Schwarzenegger and Ralf Moeller (German bodybuilding champion and star of the TV series *Conan: The Adventurer*). Whether she trains out of her own gym, someone else's gym, or her home, Laura's passion is to always give 100 percent to her clients. Laura left Hawaii in 2009 to return to her roots in New York.